The Pocket Guide

Travel Book Series

ISBN 1-86500-140-6
1. Title: The Pocket Guide to The Red Centre
Book Design: David Kirkland
Text: David Kirkland
Photography: David Kirkland. (www.kirklandphotos.com)
Scanning: Christina and Tim Nemeth, TT Digital
Proofing: A cast of thousands, then John Sims
Illustration: Malcolm Lindsay

First Printed March, 2001

Published by Hema Maps Pty Ltd
P.O Box 4365 Eight Mile Plains
Brisbane, Queensland. Australia 4113
Phone: 61 7 3340 0000
Fax: 617 33400099
E-Mail: manager@hemamaps.com.au
Web: www.hemamaps.com.au

The Pocket Guide to
The Red Centre

by

David Kirkland

THE RED CENTRE

Location: Central Australia – the Red Centre – is a tourism region in the Northern Territory which extends roughly from Alice Springs north to the Devils Marbles, south to the South Australian border, west to the Western Australia border and east to the Simpson Desert.

Primary centre: Alice Springs is the primary centre, located about 1500 kilometres south of Darwin, the capital of the Northern Territory.

Air access: Regular air access is provided from major centres to Alice Springs and Uluru (Ayers Rock).

Primary road access: The Red Centre straddles the Stuart Highway which runs north-south across the Northern Territory.

Note: The illustrative maps in this publication are representational only. For accurate, detailed guidance ask for The Red Centre Map by Hema Maps.

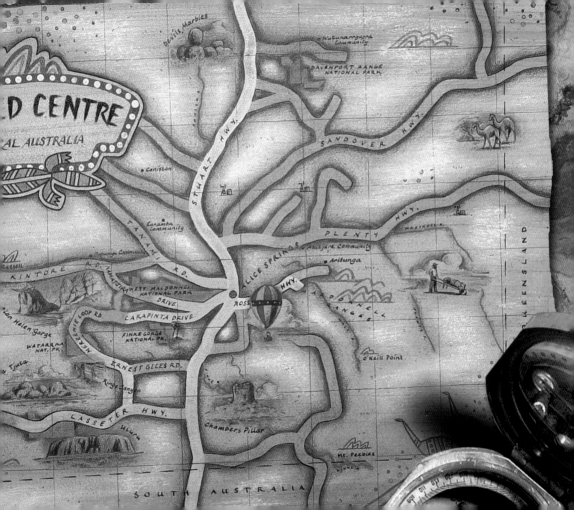

Dedicated to the pioneers of Central Australia

Contents

INTRODUCTION

So you're visiting Australia's Red Centre and you want to know what there is to see and do. Time, money and interest are all likely to make you selective but the last thing you want to feel at the end of your adventure is that you've missed anything.

Well, I'd like to think you've come to the right book.

I should point out from the outset that this book is not meant to be a definitive guide to Central Australia; it's an introduction – a traveller's companion – with plenty of photographs to help you decide where to go, a balanced reference to the best places to visit, helpful maps and information on subjects I think might interest you during your trip. It also has some entertaining yarns, a few tips and some reading suggestions for those who want to journey beyond the limits of this book.

For me – and I suspect for many Australians – the journey to Uluru invariably becomes a pilgrimage. In my case, it found me searching to define what it is to be Australian. It didn't start out that way – it was more of a holiday with a book in the making – but it became increasingly so the closer I got to the Rock. Maybe it was a consequence of the forced introspection that came with the long drive from Queensland; maybe it was the remoteness of the interior which seemed to exaggerate the Australian character in the people I met; maybe it was simply the answer I gave myself to the singular question which everyone invariably asks: "Why am I travelling thousands of kilometres to stand before a rock in the middle of the Australian desert?"

But, as I soon discovered, a trip to the Centre is far more than driving a long way to see a rock – it's a journey into the heart and soul of Australia. And what you can expect when you get there goes a long way towards defining what it is to be Australian and what makes Australia unique as a nation.

It's the little things I couldn't help noticing, the things I'd been too busy to see in the cities, the things I'd failed to appreciate about Australia even when I was abroad. It's the raised finger on the steering wheel of the oncoming car acknowledging a shared experience or promising assistance if need be; it's tuning in to local talkback radio and listening to the "battlers" from the bush; it's stopping at an outback pub for a counter meal and a beer (the Olympic pole vaulting was on the overhead TV. Said one of the old timers: "I haven't been that high since I tried to jump the electric fence."); it's sitting around the campfire trying to explain to foreign travellers that "bastard" can be a term of endearment, or the meaning of words like "Chocka", "Ocka", "Wobbly" and "Onyamate".

For me, the journey to the Centre was about reading of the great explorers who opened up the interior and feeling a sense of pride in their accomplishment; it was about travelling across this vast country and experiencing the space which is so unfathomable, even terrifying, to many visitors who come to our shores and venture inland; it was about gaining an insight into the colourful, often challenging, lifestyles of the people who choose to live in the Centre; it was about how I came to recognise – and quietly celebrate – our sometimes peculiar sense of humour (why is it we tend to ridicule most those closest to us?) and the values we pride ourselves on – mateship, a fair go and hard work.

For me, travelling the Centre was all about marvelling at the natural features that attract people from all over the world and claiming them as my own. It was learning, first hand, about Aboriginal culture and taking the time to understand how we have come to share this country and the responsibilities which are ahead of us.

Travelling the Centre is all about the exceptional experiences: of floating high above the Australian desert in a hot air balloon or traversing its ancient riverbeds by foot, camel or car; of sampling bush tucker – honey ant, witchetty grub and kangaroo; of bathing in pristine waterholes carved into mountain ranges millions of years old; of seeing the stars of the night sky clearer than I'd ever recalled seeing them before; of sitting down to a silver service meal in the middle of the desert and watching the dwindling light fall on Uluru and Kata Tjuta in the distance.

And, importantly, it's about outback – right outback – adventure.

Of course, it's impossible to consider the Red Centre without Uluru.

For me it was a profound experience to stand at the base of Uluru and bask in its timeless majesty and presence – much more than words can convey, much more than any photograph is likely to capture. You simply need to experience Uluru to know what I'm talking about.

But what makes Uluru and the Centre special is what comes afterwards, when you get home to share your stories of adventure. It's then you realise that while Uluru was probably the main reason you went to the Centre, its greatest gift was actually the journey you took to see it.

A TOWN LIKE ALICE

With a population of about 30,000, Alice Springs has grown to become a modern town and a great place to base yourself when you're exploring Central Australia. While it has enough attractions of its own to warrant several days just wandering around (for more details, stop in at Central Australian Tourism on Gregory Terrace), its appeal to visitors is that most of the Centre's main attractions are within just a day's drive – north, south, east or west. If you're visiting the region for a couple of weeks, it's worth investing some time in finding comfortable accommodation at the start so you can return to it in between excursions. There are 24 hour supermarkets, a variety of restaurants for when the old camp cooking begins wearing thin, showers, laundries and some great little outdoor cafes and bars to catch up on that long- awaited refreshment.

Left: Overlooking Alice Springs from Anzac Hill.

As if to challenge the perception it may be devoid of culture, Alice also has a proliferation of art galleries, theatres, an excellent cultural precinct, and a well-stocked (air conditioned) library near the council office if you want to do some background reading.

Alice, as you quickly discover, is a fairly laid-back sort of place. Named after the wife of Charles Todd, who was responsible for laying the Overland Telegraph Line, it began as a telegraph station back in the late 1800s, took on the mantle of the administrative centre for the region and has largely been growing around tourism ever since (Alice now receives upwards of 450,000 tourists a year). Whether you're in Alice to stop for a few weeks or you're just passing through, you can expect a pleasant respite from whatever lengthy journey you're likely to have taken to get there.

The settling of Alice

The Arrernte Aborigines were the first to inhabit the area now known as Alice Springs some 20,000 years ago (Back then it was called Mparntwe). White settlement followed the arrival of the surveyor John McDouall Stuart in 1860. Since then – according to the plaque overlooking Alice Springs on Anzac Hill (from where the photo on the previous page was taken) – the following dates have proved significant:

1871 Telegraph station built at the Alice Springs waterhole as part of the Overland Telegraph Line.

1877 Arrival of Lutheran missionaries

1887 Gold rush at Arltunga

1967 38,000 tourists arrive in Alice.

1976 Federal legislation passed granting Aboriginal people land rights.

1978 Northern Territory granted self-government.

Right: Section of the stained-glass window at the Alice Springs Cultural Precinct. Designed by Wenten Rubuntja, interpreted by Jenny Green.

Alice Springs Desert Park

Turning up for a travelling holiday in Central Australia without any understanding of the desert is like walking into an art gallery with no idea what you're looking at. Simply put, the experience is likely to be much richer if you know at least a little about what surrounds you.

There's a lot to learn and – in my opinion – much to be enjoyed about the desert after a visit to the Alice Springs Desert Park on the outskirts of the town.

Now I know there's the initial hurdle of "But why would I come so far to see an artificial desert when I'm within cooee of the real thing?" And it's an additional expense. But the reality is – unless you have the blood and patience of David Attenborough coursing through your veins (and he, for one, couldn't praise the park more highly when he visited) – you're unlikely to stay long enough, travel far enough or simply be lucky enough to see many of the elements of the desert in their

full splendour during your visit. So what the desert park does very successfully is condense many different desert habitats and features into one area and combines it with a knowledgeable, user-friendly interpretation which allows you to wander off into the Centre later and apply that newfound knowledge for yourself.

The park has several distinct habitats brimming with flora in various stages of their cycles. There are also specially designed viewing enclosures for many rare desert species and some impressive demonstrations from the big birds of prey. In short, it's well worth the entrance fee.

Above: Australia's largest lizard, the perentie. **Right:** One of several distinct desert habitats you'll see at the Alice Springs Desert Park.

BUYING A DOT PAINTING

It's been about 30 years since a young Sydney art teacher introduced acrylic paints to his students at the Papunya Aboriginal community, just west of Alice Springs, sparking an art movement which propelled the richness of a 40,000-year-old culture onto canvas. Since then, art in Central Australia has become a multimillion dollar industry which earns an income for hundreds of Aboriginal artists in remote communities throughout the Western Desert region.

However, long before it manifested itself into what is now popularly referred to as dot painting, art was an important means by which the Aboriginal people of the region communicated and strengthened their spiritual ties with the land and their culture. Laying patterns of sand on the ground in time-honoured rituals, etching Dreamtime symbols into rock faces and evoking their spiritual ancestors through body art were ways in which many of the stories, patterns and symbols we see in Aboriginal art today were carried through the millennia onto a range of new mediums.

"Choosing a piece of Aboriginal art from the Centre is no different to selecting any other piece of art," says

Tim Rollason, Development Officer with Desart, an umbrella organisation based in Alice Springs which represents the interests of 35 art centres and more than 3500 artists throughout Central Australia. "As a private buyer, you need to look for things like composition, colour, technique and – most importantly – what appeals to you personally.

"The best thing you can do is familiarise yourself with a body of work – have a look at several galleries of Aboriginal art, develop a discerning eye for what you like and become familiar with the work of certain artists. Because Western Desert art is often narrative, try and talk with either the artist or the art co-ordinator in the community to learn more about the work; read. In some cases, the artists provide a story on paper of their paintings. Art coordinators work closely with the artists – often having to translate their language – to ensure the true meaning of the work is passed onto the buyer,"he says.

Dots, while popular, are only one of the styles used by the Western Desert artists who are now transferring their art to a range of mediums including textiles, pottery and glass.

The stories behind many of the works are often complex, referring symbolically to the artist's land, totems, relationships and creation stories. Colours and patterns are also significant; the permission to use them sometimes inherited only by ancient Aboriginal law.

The price of a painting can range from around $100 to more than $!0,000 for a substantial canvas of a well known artist. "Money is a secondary consideration for many of the remote community artists," says Tim, referring to what is known among the local art community as the "dots for dollar" syndrome. "Aboriginal people in remote areas will only do something if they are interested in what they are doing and if they are working in an enjoyable environment. That's why the art centres are successful. Far more important to the artists is the fact other people value their work and that they are sharing their culture with the world – it gives them, and their community, a tremendous sense of identity and pride."

And here's an idea...

Why not try doing your own dot painting while you're travelling. There's a craft shop just off the Todd Street Mall. Wander in and buy a miniature canvas (or two), a couple of tubes of acrylic paint, a brush and a box of matches (they're for the dots) then have a go. It's fun drawing ideas from the art you see in the Centre and creating your own story. Concentric circles for waterholes, crescents for camp sites, simplified patterns for the features and lines or dots for the journey. It will give you an appreciation of the skill and patience involved in making a bigger painting and – assuming you do a halfway reasonable job – it will make an attractive memento or gift.

More dots....and dashes

The laying of more than 3200 kilometres of telegraph line stretching north-south across Australia back in the 1870s was, understandably, considered quite an achievement. After all, Stuart had only just crossed the Centre. Charles Todd was given the responsibility of linking Australia to the rest of the world, which would involve standing and wiring 36,000 poles at 80 metre intervals, with repeater stations every 250 kilometres. There was the small matter of finding enough poles and transporting them, temperatures of more than 40 degrees, a lack of water one minute and flooding the next, the standard diet of tinned beef and lime juice, intense – hardly remarkable – interstate rivalry and, as if that were not enough, a financial penalty for every day its erection extended beyond the 18-month deadline. Today, the telegraph station in Alice Springs – now a museum – stands as testament to the achievement.

Right: Alice Springs Telegraph Station

The Singing Line

I found this book by journalist Alice Thomson an insightful and thoroughly enjoyable read. I can highly recommend it as a companion for people travelling the Centre. The story is a modern-day journey of discovery for the great-great-granddaughter of Alice, the wife of Charles Todd (of Telegraph Line fame) after whom Alice Springs was named. It's a beautifully crafted tale which interweaves the past and present to provide an astute, refreshing and well researched insight into Central Australia.

Alice shares a frustrating moment:

"I spent the afternoon trying to arrange a few days with some Aborigines. But their guardians were more supercilious and protective than the Buckingham Palace press office. The idea of doing a little snake hunting and lizard eating with them was as ludicrous as suggesting going hunting with the Queen."

On the white attitudes to Aborigines:
"As we wandered back into town we watched the groups of Aborigines along the dry Todd river bed surrounded by lottery tickets and cans of beer. In the Todd Street Mall they sat lethargically on the litter bins. Most of white Alice reacted in the same way whenever we mentioned the subject. First they would enthuse about the dreaming stories, and extol the virtues of the Aboriginal art in the galleries saying they were a matter of reverence and national pride, like a Turner or a Gainsborough. Then they would admit that white policies over the past two centuries had destroyed the Aborigines' independence. But get them on the present and they would open up. A small reservoir of embarrassment turned into a torrent of frustration. The two groups seemed to be ruining each other's lives."

It would have to be something special to get me out of bed at four in the morning, but there I was standing outside my hotel waiting be to picked up. On board the basket-trailing coach was our pilot, Sven, his co-pilot (though he spent the entire morning on the ground chasing after us) and the six people who would accompany me in the gondola. According to Sven we'd spend about half an hour travelling to the launch site and another half an hour attaching the balloon to the basket. In between, there'd be a couple of stops when a small helium balloon would be sent into the heavens to determine the wind direction. Said Sven, "We have a number of sites to launch the balloon from depending on which way the wind is blowing. Our flight rate is very high, about 320 days a year. The conditions this morning

Right: A blast of hot air heralds the lift-off.

look pretty good. We should be up for an hour." His prediction brought an excited murmur from the group – a nurse, a German couple who couldn't speak English and an Indian family – husband, wife and daughter – celebrating the wife's birthday. As promised, within half an hour we had all clambered into the gondola and were ducking to avoid the blasts of hot air that held the giant balloon aloft. Then, ever so gently, we lifted off, slowly rising to where we could see the sun peeking over the distant horizon and the desert landscape bathed in golden light unfolding beneath us. The Indian husband could not contain himself and chatted excitedly throughout the entire ascent – a common response, reflected Sven – while the rest of us quietly savoured the view. In the distance, we could see the MacDonnell Ranges and Alice Springs. Several other balloons had lifted off at the same time. Having reached an optimum height, we descended to just above the tree tops, casting the balloon's shadow across the spinifex covered plain. Kangaroos could be seen bounding away beneath us. "You may notice the basket doesn't have wheels," said Sven, as we came in for landing, "so you'll need to hold on." We did, though there was no real need for concern, and we ended the morning with the traditional champagne breakfast.

Not a bad way to start the day, methinks.

Left: High above the MacDonnell Ranges, with Alice in the distance.

T he people of Alice Springs pride themselves on their ability to laugh in the face of adversity and have a good time. Apparently, it's all to do with the heat, the hardship and the isolation. Hence, for the past 30 years or so – come late September, early October – up to a hundred competitors brave soaring temperatures to stage one of the most unusual river regattas in the world – The Henley-on-Todd.

What makes the annual event remarkable is that there is no water in the river. Only three times in its history has there been more than a trickle, and yet it invariably leaves in its wake a flotilla of spent vessels and exhausted competitors who race their boats – if you can call them that – up and down the sandy river bed in a bid to be immortalised in the Henley-on-Todd hall of fame (The next edition of the Centralian Advocate newspaper).

Selection criteria for the event are virtually nonexistent. The vessels – which are carried – must resemble a boat, registrations can be made on the morning of the challenge, and any money raised on the day goes to Rotarian charities. Volunteers share in the glory of the local teams; open rivalry is decided in competition or by the rule of water pistol.

The main course for the event runs over about 50 meters of Alice Springs' Todd River (that's excluding the preliminary cavalcade through the town mall), with spectators – up to 5000 tourists in a good year – crowding a cordoned section of the shaded river bank to view the full day's program. Events include the coxless eight and four which sees several teams harnessed in a flimsy frame and running barefoot around buoys of 44 gallon drums, the Oxford Sprint where competitors shovel, rather than paddle, their vessels to victory, and the day's highlight – some serious theatre with an all-out mock battle between the prides of the fleet – three battleships (frames on top of cars) which circle the arena firing water cannons and coloured flour bombs at each other.

All up, it's an entertaining desert spectacle with competitors and spectators leaving happy – and possibly hopeful that the day's events might even cause the Gods to shed a tear of laughter and bring rain to Alice's dusty old riverbed.

Right: Heading for an emergency at the Henley-on-Todd.

First contact

"People who come to the Centre expecting to see a traditional Aborigine running around in a red loin cloth with a dead kangaroo draped over his shoulder and a boomerang hanging from his waist are going to be disappointed."

– Paul Ah Chee Ngala

Most visitors arrive in the Centre expecting to come into contact with three things – Uluṟu, the desert and Aboriginal people.

While the experience of visiting Uluṟu and the desert is pretty straightforward, the contact you're likely to have with Aboriginal people can range from gaining a rich and rewarding insight into a 40,000-year-old culture to a brief, uncomfortable interlude with one of the "Todd Mall nomads".

"People who come to the Centre expecting to see a traditional Aborigine running around in a red loin cloth with a dead kangaroo draped over his shoulder and a boomerang hanging from his waist are going to be disappointed," says Paul Ah Chee Ngala, the owner of The Aboriginal Art and Culture Centre in Alice Springs.

"There's a romance associated with Aboriginal culture, and the tourism industry generally looks to promote and

Right: A popular way to experience Aboriginal culture in the Centre.

accommodate that, but visitors need to understand that is not how most Aboriginal people live."

"When visitors come to Alice Springs, they are surprised to see many Aboriginal people dressed the same way they are. They have jobs, they live in houses, they run businesses. Of course, visitors also see signs of a culture struggling with change – where traditional law is being diminished by another law, the Westminster system – but that's life. Part of the experience of coming to the Centre is putting all of that into context," he said

"Realistically, what visitors can expect when they come to Central Australia is a brief insight into traditional and contemporary Aboriginal culture. Through tours and displays they will get a glimpse of the strong bond Aboriginal people still have for their land and the effort they are making to revive their culture. They will have the opportunity to see history through the eyes of Aboriginal people and gain a firsthand insight into some of the issues now confronting both white and black Australians," he said.

With more than 50% of the Northern Territory registered as Aboriginal land, Paul says it needs to be understood that many Aboriginal communities simply don't want contact with tourists. "That's why you see the signs off the highway prohibiting entry," he said.

"Many Aboriginal people have chosen to return to their land and just want to be left alone. It's also worth bearing in mind that for many who are living in the communities, English is not their first language."

Paul says the divide between black and white is slowly being bridged. "I'm optimistic about the future of Aboriginal people. I think what's needed now is a massive effort by government to educate Aboriginal people at a very young age. We're a small and isolated country; we can do it. It will take time – at least a generation – and it won't be easy, but I think we're finally on the right track.

"In the meantime, maybe we can all benefit from being more realistic about what to expect from Aboriginal people."

The Dreamtime

A basic understanding of what is widely referred to as the Dreamtime is an important part of recognising the inextricable bond traditional Aborigines have for the land and their culture.

It can be a complex concept to grasp.

Professor Ted Strehlow (refer following story) has long been regarded as an eminent authority in the western world on Aboriginal culture and his writing on the subject in his book *Central Australian Religion* (1978) provides an excellent insight into the concept of creation, among the Arrernte speaking Aborigines of Central Australia. Drawing largely from his book, following is an introduction to the concept of the Dreamtime or Creation period which, hopefully, will go a small way to helping visitors understand the traditional belief system of Aborigines in Central Australia.

Traditional Aborigines believe the earth, like the sky, always existed and was the home of supernatural beings. At the beginning of time the earth looked like a featureless, desolate plain. Nothing existed on the surface. The earth was covered in eternal darkness as the sun and moon were still slumbering under the earth's cold crust. Only beneath the surface of the earth did life already exist in the form of thousands of supernatural beings which lay dormant, along with a vague form of human life that existed in the shape of semi-embryonic masses of half developed infants. Time began when the supernatural beings awoke and broke through the surface of the earth. The earth was soon flooded with light as the sun too rose from the ground. The supernatural beings varied greatly in appearance. Some rose in animal shapes resembling kangaroos and emus, others emerged in human guise looking like perfectly formed men and women. There was an indivisible link between humans, animals and plants. Those beings that looked like animals thought and acted like humans, and those in human form could change at will into animals. After emerging from their eternal slumber, the beings – referred to as totemic ancestors (such a Wallaby Dreaming and Emu Dreaming etc) – moved about the earth bringing into being the physical features of the landscape. Mountains, sandhills, plains and rivers all arose to mark the deeds of the wandering totemic ancestors. Not a single prominent feature was created which was not associated with an episode of the supernatural beings. The sacred songs of their deeds were compositions by the supernatural beings themselves. It was these compositions which became the subject of the many sacred myths, songs and ceremonies in which Aboriginal religious beliefs were to find expression. Hence, they were sung on ceremonial occasions and body decorations were worn by actors impersonating the totemic ancestors. All sacred ritual was regarded as eternal and unalterable.

The supernatural beings continued to roam until, exhausted by their effort, they fell back into their sleep and returned to the earth. Many vanished into the ground, often from the sites where they first emerged, others turned into physical objects like rocks or trees. The places that marked their final resting place were regarded as sacred sites to be approached only by initiated men. But before their disappearance from the face of the earth, the sun and moon and the rest of the earth-born celestial beings rose into the sky, and man was left to wander the earth.

The Strehlow Research Centre

It's a measure of the high regard with which Professor Ted Strehlow was held that Arrernte Aboriginal elders invited him to document their culture to preserve the knowledge and customs which they feared would otherwise die with them. That was back in the 1930's. Since then, Professor Strehlow went on to amass a huge collection of artifacts and documents which continues to be stored for safekeeping at the Strehlow Research Centre. The collection comprises more than a thousand sacred ceremonial objects, 800 documented ceremonies and hundreds of hours of film and audio footage, photographs and published material – many of which, in keeping with the wishes of the people who have entrusted their knowledge to the centre – may never be seen by the general public. In a time when we are only beginning to come to terms with the richness of Aboriginal culture and are recognising how much of it has been destroyed in the name of progress, the Strehlow Research Centre provides a valuable resource for future generations – black and white.

A few short trips out of Alice

There are several popular day trips north and south out of Alice, including the Ewaninga Rock Carvings, Rainbow Valley, the Henbury Meteorite Crater and the Devils Marbles. While you're likely to visit at least one of the attractions on your way into Alice (that's assuming you're driving), here's a round-up of what you can expect from the others.

Ewaninga Rock Carvings (right) are about 30 kilometres south of Alice. It's a pleasant enough drive, though the road is unsealed. While the petroglyphs are interesting (that's assuming you haven't seen an Aboriginal petroglyph before), a fair bit is left to the imagination as the meaning of the symbols according to Arrernte elders is too dangerous to reveal to people not initiated into Aboriginal law. **Rainbow Valley** (following page) – about 75 kilometres south along the Stuart Highway and a short drive inland along a four-wheel-drive track – makes for a good photograph (the flies aren't always that bad). There are camping facilities and it's best to get there mid-afternoon so you have time to explore before sunset lights up the sandstone cliffs. If you've got a bit of time to spare, drop into **Stuarts Well** for some camel contact (refer story page 46). Another 50 kilometres or so - the last 13 on an unsealed road - takes you to **Henbury Meteorite Crater** to see what a piece of space debris the size of a 44 gallon drum can do when it crashes to earth at 44,000 kilometres an hour. The actual meteor is long gone – spirited away by souvenir hunters and museums – but, if nothing else, you'll leave knowing the difference between a meteor and a meteorite. (alright, alright, a meteorite is a meteorite until it lands on earth, when it becomes a meteor).

If you're looking for something north of Alice, **The Devils Marbles** are the obvious choice (refer stories page 52-54).

Right: The Ewaninga Rock Carvings.

"BLOODY FLIES!"

Spawned by the millions in cow dung, engineered to outrun and outmanoeuvre a human being in flight, instinctively programmed to track us down by our mucus, saliva and blood, and bred with a single mission in life – to drive us to the brink of despair. Allow me to introduce the humble Musca vetustissima – commonly referred to as the ##@@!!! Australian bush fly.

By now, assuming you've arrived in Central Australia during the summer months and spent a few days camping, I'm sure there's no need for introductions to this most persistent of pests. It's our protein that attracts them, I'm told. The females in particular need it to develop their ovaries, and once they leave their comfortable cow pat (though kangaroo or human doo will do), nothing makes the irritating mites happier than dragging themselves through a bit of mucus, swimming in a pool of saliva, traipsing over an open wound or diving into a moist part of the human body.

While normally I'd swat investigation of such annoyances aside, given that next to Ulu_ru – certainly in summer – the bush fly is likely to be the most common subject of conversation around the desert campfire, I thought you might be interested in these few snippets:

• Bush flies – unlike house flies, horse flies or blow flies – live primarily on dung (which should bring some comfort to all of us who have inadvertently swallowed them).

Left: Rainbow Valley – the sunlit cliffs make up for the flies you're likely to get in the summer months.

43

• We're outnumbered. Bush flies breed largely in cow pats. Australia has about 20 million cattle, each of which drops an average 12 pats of dung a day. From a single cow pat, an estimated 2000 bush flies can emerge. (by my calculation, that leaves the Australian population outnumbered by at least 240,000 to one).

• The bush fly is at its irritating worst at temperatures of between 28 and 35 degrees.

• Bush flies don't fly at under 12 degrees, they settle at sunset and roost on the end of leaves and twigs at night.

• The average life span of a bush fly ranges from two weeks to two months depending on the temperature (and your aim).

• Bush flies travel at about 8km/h under their own steam but can reach speeds of about 20 km/h when wind assisted.

• Bush flies can begin mating when they're three days old.

• They are a permanent blight on the Australian landscape. While they do not survive southern Australian winters, they continue to breed in the north and migrate south as the cold retreats, covering much of the continent by the end of summer.

• The natural enemies of the bush fly (apart from irate humans) are some species of birds, dragonflies, wasps and beetles.

• The closest science has come to containing bushfly numbers is through the introduction of dung beetles (40 exotic species have been introduced to Australia), which bury the dung and therefore prevent the flies from breeding (given the flies that remain, I can only assume there are not enough dung beetles).

• Since the earliest explorers, the anguish suffered from bushflies has been vigorously recorded, many citing as frustratingly ineffective an assortment of eye drops, fly veils, lures and repellents.

• Bush legend has it the most successful answer to the bush fly problem was devised by a Queensland inventor from Bedourie who created the "Bedourie Fly Trap". The bushman's remedy was to cut a hole in the seat of his trousers.

"No language could convey the slightest idea of the agonies suffered through these pests, or the awful blasphemy they are responsible for."

– Allan Davidson, 1898

CAMEL CRUSADE

I should begin by confessing that I have gone out of my way to publish the most ridiculous photograph of Bundy I could find. It is – I regret – all that I can do to exact some small measure of revenge on this seemingly hapless beast for the state of my backside after seven hours in the saddle. Added to this was the humiliation I suffered believing that the person holding the reins – as opposed to the camel with them dangling from his nose peg - was the one in charge.

I'd travelled about an hour and a half south from Alice Springs to join 10 other people for the last day of a seven day trek out of Stuarts Well. "I've done plenty of horse riding so it shouldn't take me long to get the hang of it," I'd assured my hosts at Alice Springs Camel Outback Safaris, who pointed out that unlike other companies, their camels were not tied in a line and trailed, but were independently reined, enabling riders to spread out.

Like most people, I quickly succumbed to the charms of the desert dromedary (that's one hump not two) – the long, eyelashes, the soft, whiskered snout, that cute, docile expression that begs affection. Then there's the history and associated romance of the camel ride – watching the country unfold from a camel's back as it did for our early explorers; being carried aloft through the red, spinifex covered sandhills by these majestic ships of the desert.

Having been introduced to Bundy, the seduction continued as this huge, gangly beast crumbled submissively to its knees in front of me so I could climb onto its back. This was followed by the cursory glance over its shoulder as if to make sure I was alright after we'd risen, and the gentle swaying that lulls you into a sense of false security. In return – I suspect like most first-time riders – my affection for Bundy grew and I was moved to reassure him with regular pats and whispers of being in the hands of a firm but fair master. The apparent nods of agreement coming from up front were testament enough

that a special bond had been created between man and beast, I concluded – and, with that, I sat back satisfied that we'd got off to a good start.

It was after about an hour in the saddle (at about the point where it's too far to get off and walk back) that things began to change. The understanding I thought I had about who is in charge, well, all that dissipated faster than water in the desert. It started something like this: "Wait a minute, Bundy, I didn't direct you towards that bush so you could get a mouthful. Hey, Bundy, I didn't pull on the reins for you to stop here, and hey, Bundy, I didn't encourage you to slow down – in fact mate, I think we need to speed up to catch the rest. Bundy...Bundy, c'mon, let's go."

A pitiful performance ensued as I tried to exert my will over this denizen of the desert. My plight was accentuated by the fact that with all the commotion, my fellow cameleers had returned hoping to be entertained by

Left: A camel's eye view.

what would have been a concentrated replay of what they'd each gone through over the past six days.

I began by digging my heels into Bundy's side and making encouraging cameleer-type-phrases like "Trot it up" and "Hooshta" -- but to no avail. Then came the piece of garden hose I'd been given and the smacks across the rump. But still nothing. In fact, it occurred to me that apart from fuelling my own frustration, my comic efforts had done little more than stimulate Bundy's appetite.

It was at this juncture I should have heeded the advice of those around me and just sat back to enjoy the ride, resigned to the fact that Bundy would invariably follow the other camels and make his way back in his own good time. But no, having brought my fellow cameleers to fits of laughter, I had elected to salvage what little dignity remained by showing Bundy who was boss. He was, after all, only a camel, I reasoned. With that I launched into a Yeeeeeeeehaaaaa that would have driven bison herds across a continent and followed with a frantic combination of blows from heel and hose. All this while rapidly rising and falling piston-like in my saddle. It was a performance even Bundy couldn't ignore. Drawing stationary, he turned and gazed around at me with that cud-chewing expression that says, "You can't be serious", regurgitated a palate of leaves, burped dismissively and turned to drift in the direction he was going before I'd interrupted him.

And I've got to say I tried several times to spur Bundy into action, each ending the same way – with me collapsing after a few minutes, spent and cussing in the saddle. I should add that Bundy did canter, in fact more than once, though generally it was at his whim rather than at my instruction, and it was often orientated towards low-hanging branches. Any extended bursts lasted just long enough for me to begin to gain a sense of rhythm. Then he promptly stopped.

It was somewhere in between realising my futile pounding had reduced the cheeks of my backside to the thickness of the saddle flaps and

Right: A shadow of my former self.

convincing myself that Bundy was now deriving considerable pleasure from my plight that I decided to give up and save myself from further ignominy. Sadly, however, this proved not to be the case. Several hours later, with our destination clearly in sight and me desperate to flee the saddle, Bundy celebrated my final gasp of resistance by wandering into a deep puddle in front of a bus load of tourists and sat down amid what quickly became a barrage of humiliating camera flashes.

Footnote: Despite my carry-on, I reckon riding a camel is a great way to experience the Centre (though obviously I'd recommend early capitulation to the camel unless you know what you're doing and I'd be chucking in some serious padding for good measure). The pace and height allow you to appreciate the desert from a completely different perspective and you get a feel (now there's an understatement) for what it must have been like for our early explorers.

There are several camel tour operators in the Centre. Rides vary from a half-hour wander through to a 14-day safari. For further details contact Central Australian Tourism.

"It was somewhere in between realising my futile pounding had reduced the cheeks of my backside to the thickness of the saddle flaps and convincing myself that Bundy was now deriving considerable pleasure from my plight that I decided to give up and save myself from further ignominy."

By any other name...

There are several Aboriginal names given to the tourist highlights of the Centre which you're best to learn – and pronounce – right from the start, as they appear frequently in books, signage, magazines and conversation. Ignore them, as I discovered, and they're likely to taunt you throughout your journey.

ULURU — (Ayers Rock). Pronounced OO-LA-ROO. The name of the Rock you've come so far to see.

TJUKURPA — Pronounced CHOOK-OOR-PA. You'll hear a lot of this around Uluru. It's the law which governs the lives of traditional aborigines living at Uluru.

KATA TJUTA — (The Olgas). Pronounced KAT-A-JEW-TA. Those other rocks next to Uluru.

ANANGU — Pronounced AN-ANG -GOO. Is the name of the Aborigines who live around Uluru.

YULARA — Pronounced YOO-LA-RA. The resort village that services Uluru.

ARRERNTE — Pronounced ARE-ENT-EE. The traditional Aborigines of Alice Springs.

WATARRKA — Pronounced WAT-AR-KA. It's Kings Canyon National Park.

The Devils Marbles

Depending on who you're talking to, the Devils Marbles are either a fascinating geological phenomenon, the eggs of the mythological Rainbow Serpent, or landing beacons for UFOs.

If you're listening to stories of the latter, you'll hear of white lights zig-zagging the skyline and chasing cars along the Stuart Highway, a conspiracy between aliens and the military, and beams of light drawing tourists towards spaceships (refer following story).

The Devils Marbles are part of a 1800 hectare conservation reserve located about 400 kilometres north of Alice Springs and, regardless of who you're talking to, they make an interesting stopover.

Where the term Devils Marbles originated from, no one seems to know (though I think it was a great marketing ploy, myself). The closest anyone seems be to be able to get is a reference by a surveyor involved in the construction of the Overland Telegraph back in 1872.

To the untrained eye, the conservation reserve is an undulating landscape strewn with large round boulders – many precariously balanced on top of oneanother – and a great opportunity for a photograph. Wander the reserve and you're bound to find some formation which takes your fancy.

Geologically, the Devils Marbles began as giant blocks created when fault lines divided a massive plate of granite about 1600 million years ago. Over time, extremes in temperature combined with water and erosion to cause the characteristic onion-like peeling – or exfoliation – which reduced and honed the blocks to the rounded

boulders we see today.

Local Aborigines have their own interpretation of the site, believing the boulders were created by a giant mythological snake which carved out the landscape. The boulders, which they call Karlwekarlwe (meaning round objects) are believed to be the eggs of the Rainbow Serpent – one of the central figures in Aboriginal Dreamtime stories. The land on which the boulders sit is regarded as a sacred site. Stories are still told among its Aboriginal custodians about Dreamtime creatures that inhabit the earth beneath the surface.

TOP TIP Best to arrive a couple of hours before sunset to give you time to wander the landscape and find that special backdrop for a photo or decide whether you want to stay over at the campsite. If you arrive around midday when it's hot and the light is stark, you can expect to be less impressed.

LITTLE GREEN MEN IN THE RED CENTRE

It's hard not to notice Lou's place at Wycliffe Well. Follow the Stuart Highway south a short distance from the Devils Marbles, glance out of your car window to the right, and you'll see a service station with two aliens and a spaceship parked out the front. Lou Farkas is the Northern Territory's resident UFO expert – the one the media call when there's been another sighting. Catch him in a quiet moment and Lou brims with stories of all things extra-terrestrial. "This, after all, is where the earth's energy fields intersect, which is what attracts them," he assures me. A 10 minute chat with Lou sees him looking you straight in the eye and telling stories about the spaceship that came so close he could see the windows on the side, strange lights that chased cars off the road, guests who have been drawn by spaceship lights, conspiracy theories to rival the X-Files and the weird people all this UFO publicity has attracted. He has one yarn about a woman who arrived claiming to be associated with an international UFO organisation. She stayed in one of his cabins. When the cleaner went to do her room the next morning she pushed open to door to find the woman levitating above her bed. She later left, leaving an assortment of strange hieroglyphics – possibly warnings – painted on the wall. Now Lou says he doesn't chase publicity and prefers to keep a low profile, which sort of explains all the alien paintings round the place and the green couple with the spaceship posing out the front, so, if you're planning to drop in, you need to be aware that not everyone is likely to receive an audience.

Still, his visitor guest book makes interesting reading and after perusing some of the comments you have to wonder how so many other people can all be getting it wrong.

Previous page and left: The Devils Marbles. **Right:** Resident UFO expert Lou Farkas.

Great travelling companions from a distant past

If you're into history and like a good read, the adventures and journals of Stuart, Gosse and Giles – three of the Centre's most intrepid early explorers – provide excellent background reading for your visit to the Centre. (Try the Alice Springs Library, or a few second-hand book shops before you leave).

John McDouall Stuart was the first to make it to the Centre and went on to cross the entire continent from south to north. His journals are a dry, though fascinating, read as they capture the immediacy of his hardship, and you'll be able to relate to his last trip as you're speeding along the Stuart Highway in your air conditioned car.

William Gosse, the first to reach Uluṟu, penned brief notes which were tabled in parliament and, while again dry, his first impressions of Uluru also make interesting reading.

But it was Ernest Giles who wrote most eloquently of the Centre. His journals or his subsequent book make an excellent literary companion, particularly if you're visiting Finke Gorge National Park, Uluṟu, Kata Tjuṯa and Kings Canyon.

Here are some excerpts from their writings:

Stuart's hardship:

• *"On return to my camp I shall have intervals of 60 and 80 miles to pass over on which there will not now be a drop of water, and yet it remains to be proved whether or not my retreat is altogether cut off"* Stuart had to turn back just 500 miles from the Centre.

• *"I am now reduced to a perfect skeleton, a mere shadow…I can chew nothing, and all that I have been living on is a little beef tea, and a little boiled flour."* Towards the end of his final journey.

Gosse's impressions of Uluṟu:

• *"This Rock is certainly the most wonderful natural feature I have ever seen. It appears more wonderful every time I look at it and I may say, it is a sight worth riding over 84 miles of spinifex sandhills to see."*

• *"This seems to be a favourite resort of the natives in the wet season judging from the numerous camps in every cave."*

Giles on the Olgas

"They have stood as huge memorials of the

ancient times of earth, for ages, countless eons of ages, since. The rocks are smoothed with the attrition of the alchemy of years. Time, the old, the dim musician has ineffectually laboured here, although with all the powers of an ocean at his command."

Giles lamenting his companion's solid sleeping habits and the ants:

• *"I could not help moralising (as I stood near him considering his peace and placidity) upon our different mental and physical conditions: here was one human being, young and strong certainly, sleeping away the dreary hours of the night, regaining the necessary vigour for the toils of the coming day, totally oblivious to swarms of insects that not only crawled over him but kept constantly biting his flesh; while another, who perhaps prided himself too much on the mental gifts bestowed by God upon him, was compelled by the same insects to wander through the whole night from rock to rock and place to place unable to remain for more than a moment anywhere."*

Responding to a spear throwing attack by an irate Aborigine on Christmas Day who retreated behind a rock and launched a diatribe on his party.

• *"It appeared to me however, that this harangue*

required punctuation: so I showed him the rifle again, whereupon he immediately indulged in a full stop."

On the plight of Aborigines:

•*" The Great Designer of the Universe in the long past periods of creation, permitted a fiat to be recorded that the beings whom it was His pleasure in the first instance to place amidst these lovely scenes, must eventually be swept from the face of the earth by others more intellectual, more dearly beloved and gifted than they. Progressive improvement is undoubtedly the order of creation, and we perhaps in our turn, may be as ruthlessly driven from earth by another race of yet unknown beings of an order infinitely higher- infinitely more beloved than we."*

RECOMMENDED READING

W.C Gosse's Explorations 1873 (Parliamentary Paper).

To the Inland Sea – Charles Stuart's Expedition 1844-45 by Edward Stokes.

Geographic Travels in Central Australia by Ernest Giles.

Australia Twice Traversed by Ernest Giles.

The west MacDonnell Ranges

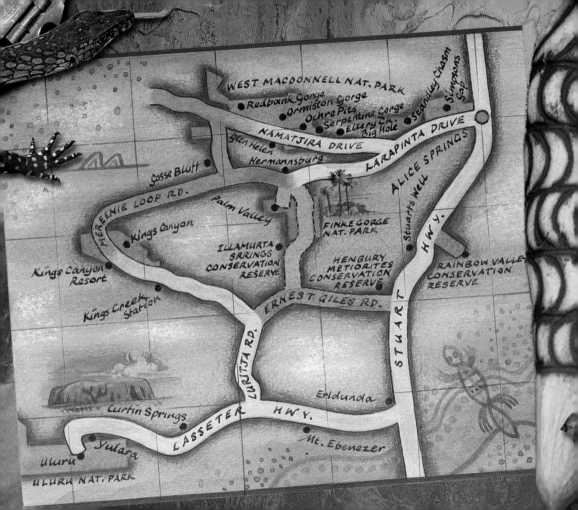

Introduction to
"The West Macs"

The west MacDonnell Ranges, or "West Macs" as they're affectionately called, combine impressive gorge and mountain scenery with deep swimming holes, panoramic views, a bit of history and the opportunity to experience some Aboriginal culture. Given Glen Helen Gorge, which marks the sealed end of Namatjira Drive, is only 130 kilometres from Alice, you can plan on a pleasant day trip to any of the gorges, a comfortable five-day explore that takes in all the features of the Western Macs and James Range, or the prelude to an off-road adventure that can lead on to Kings Canyon, Palm Valley or beyond.

If you're in for the short haul, you need to bear in mind that Larapinta Drive, which deviates south to the James Range, and Namatjira Drive split about 50 kilometres out of Alice, and are joined at the other end by an unsealed road, so you'll have to double back if you want to get it all in -- that's unless you're in a four-wheel-drive of course. Regardless of which way you go, you'll be taking in some impressive countryside.

Right: The towering walls of Standley Chasm.

Namatjira Drive

First stop along Namatjira Drive is the grave of **John Flynn**, the founder of the Royal Flying Doctor Service. Then it's on to **Simpsons Gap** which – with its steep walls, river gums, swimming holes, picnic tables and light walks – is a pleasant introduction to the gorges of the "West Macs". **Standley Chasm** (previous page), named after the Centre's first schoolteacher, is further along, though it's about 20 kilometres off the highway and it's not a part of the national park so there's an entrance fee involved. Called Angkale by its Aboriginal owners, the narrow gorge is at its most impressive an hour

Left: Ellery Creek Big Hole. **Right:** Ormiston Gorge.

either side of midday when its sheer 20 metre walls light up and change colours due to reflecting sunlight. The kilometre walk along the riverbed to the gorge is pleasant enough and there's an enjoyable climb over the rocks among the cycads at the other end. Be warned though if you've come in search of solitude, the buses come around midday.

It's just beyond Standley Chasm that you have to make a choice about what you want to see next. Assuming it's gorges, stay on Namatjira as Ellery Creek Big Hole, Serpentine Gorge, Ormiston Gorge, Glen Helen Gorge and Redbank Gorge all have waterholes and pleasant sand banks to sit on. Only Serpentine and Redbank require a bit of a walk. **Ellery Creek Big Hole** is your first stop for a dip. As the closest pool to Alice it's a popular swimming spot for locals so I'd get there early. Further on is **Serpentine Gorge,** which I wouldn't overlook if you have a bit of time to wander, particularly if you want to escape the crowd (there's gravel and a 1.3 kilometre walk up the riverbed involved). There's a secluded waterhole further into the gorge and the short, steep climb above affords commanding views over the surrounding

countryside as you sit beneath the whispering branches of a lone desert oak. You can also drive on to explore **Serpentine Ruins** while you're there, which proved to be an unlikely spot for a tourism adventure, though it's interesting none-the-less, and there are camp sites if you want to sleep out.

Back out on the highway and further along are the easily accessible **Ochre Pits** from where Aborigines once extracted a variety of ochres for ritual body decorations. Visually it's not much in the extreme light of day but there's some interesting information displayed, and it's worth a peek-a-boo when the afternoon sun begins to colour the walls.

Ormiston Gorge which is grand in scale compared with the other gorges of the Western Macs is 26 kilometres further on. We're talking big, permanent, shaded waterhole, panoramic views from the gorge summit, glowing coloured cliff faces and some seriously enjoyable clambering over rocks deep into the valley. There are several walks from Ormiston Gorge (I can recommend the 1.5 hour Ghost Gum Walk), the most popular for enthusiasts being the 7 kilometre Pound Walk. **Glen Helen Gorge** and homestead marks the end of the sealed road and provides a welcomed break from the day's activities. Facing out towards a massive sheer rock wall and overlooking a pristine waterhole, the homestead provides accommodation, food and cool drinks. (It's also the base for an excellent chopper flight

Left and right: A helicopter perspective over Glen Helen Gorge and the surrounding landscape.

over features such as Ormiston Gorge, The Pound, Mount Sonder and, of course, Glen Helen Gorge itself.

Redbank Gorge (right) is the last of the public gorges out this way. There's about 20 kilometres of dirt road to travel but don't let that, or the 20 minute walk up the dry river bed, deter you. Personally, I'd plan to camp out. There's a deep waterhole at the gorge and a crevice in the rock that promises some serious adventure. Sadly, when I was there, the water was too cold to venture into, I was without something to float on, and my camera equipment did not handle too well the threat of immersion. However, in the words of another...I'll be back.

Assuming you're in a four-wheel-drive (or you have less regard for the two-wheel drive vehicle you're travelling in), you can continue for about an hour along the unsealed road, passing the Mereenie Loop Road turnoff and onto Hermannsburg. The lookout at **Tylers Pass** provides a good view over the 5 kilometre crater which was left when a comet crashed to earth millions of years ago (If you want to go and explore it, you'll need a permit beforehand (Glen Helen Homestead has them). From there, you'll have to make up your mind whether it's onto Hermannsburg and Palm Valley or you want to take the Mereenie Loop Road to Kings Canyon and on to Uluru (Page 77).

Right: Redbank Gorge.

Hunting with
THE LADIES

Important rule number one: when you're out hunting with "The Ladies", do not – under any circumstances – swerve to miss the goanna.

It was unfortunate start to my initiation into hunting with three Aboriginal artists from Haasts Bluff in the Western Desert. Alice, Linda and Eunice - had invited me hunting and we'd all bundled into my car with carrying cans, digging sticks (one metre crowbars) and water to head to a favoured hunting ground.

As we sped along the dirt track, the ladies were chatting excitedly in their language and it occurred to me that few things would have made them more animated than the prospect of a successful hunt… that was until a goanna wandered across our path and I swerved to miss it.

Alice – in the front – was the first to

respond, beginning with wild excitement when she saw the goanna on the track in front of us. What followed was total disbelief and pandemonium as I swerved to miss it. When the other ladies realised what had happened they all started pointing back and yelling for me to stop; Eunice all but left the car before I'd even wrenched on the handbrake, then all of them set off into the desert in rapid pursuit only to return a few minutes later, well, goanna-less. Now let me tell you, dear reader, the last thing you want to do is travel in a car with a group of Aboriginal women when you're the one responsible for letting the goanna get away. Silent, bodies pointing forward, eyes locked on the distant horizon, not a word was said for the rest of the journey.

However, all this, I'm happy to report, abated and I was welcomed back into the fold the minute we arrived at the hunting ground – an expanse of charred mulga desert landscape still smoking from a recent fire which I presume had been deliberately lit. The ladies quickly assumed a search pattern and were soon sitting around holes digging up the lizards that had obviously retreated to escape the flames.

Alice (pictured right) was the most productive – six goannas in a couple of hours. She just dug around the holes, reached in, grabbed the lizard's tail and then – in a single motion – ripped it out, whip lashed it in the air and pounded it on the ground before setting off for the next. Shrieks of delight across the desert punctuated each new catch. A cooking fire was soon started and the lizards were rolled in the ashes. Chatting away, we all had a meal (it's a bit like chicken really) then the women packed into carry cans what they couldn't eat and we headed back to the community.

*****

Kate Podger is the Ikuntji community art co-ordinator living at Haasts Bluff, a remote Aboriginal community about 200 kilometres from Alice. She provides support and technical advice to about 17 Aboriginal painters - all women, five of whom are "major artists". The price for their work ranges from $200 for a new artist to up to $12,000 a painting by a well-known artist. According to Kate, most of the money the women make goes towards food: "Generally, the money from the sale of their painting is eaten," says

Kate. "They buy food first, then what's left goes towards things like transport – a car is huge status in the communities – and clothing. While their art has afforded them some comforts, because they share their wealth among relatives, the artists haven't got much to show for it. Narputta, for example – one of the community's most successful artists – lives here in a three bedroom government house with 15 other people. She has a room with a bed and a cross on the wall. That's it. And she's well off; she just bought a fridge."

According to Kate, the artists produce about 12 paintings a year – the more prolific can produce up to 40. "Their happiest times are when they are hunting and telling stories. They go out into their country and come back ready to paint up a storm. The bush inspires them and they enjoy sharing their culture through their stories and paintings. Quite simply, they love it, it's what defines them."

Right: Taking a break outside the Ikuntji Women's Centre.
Far Right: Haasts Bluff artist Daisy Napaltjarri with one of her works.

Larapinta Drive

Larapinta Drive, as you'll quickly discover, leads to Namatjira country – the lavender, spinifex covered hills that provided inspiration for one of the country's most famous Aboriginal artists, Albert Namatjira. It's also the road you take to get to Hermannsburg - the first Central Australian outpost for the Lutheran mission, and the Finke River National Park.

Assuming you're coming from Alice and have just turned off Namatjira Drive, the only place of interest before Hermannsburg is **Wallace Rockhole**, about 17 kilometres along a reasonable, unsealed road. Built near a permanent waterhole, the pristine community has embraced tourism and provides cultural excursions to nearby Aboriginal sites. A small store also sells art, produced by local Aborigines.

Left: Hermannsburg Community kids at Palm Valley.

Back on Larapinta Drive, past **Namatjira's Monument** (you'd think someone would come up with something more appropriate than a "chimney"), it's onto **Hermannsburg** and the historic precinct of restored, whitewashed buildings that were built when Lutheran missionaries settled the area back in 1877.

This was also where Albert Namatjira was born and you'll find an art gallery in the precinct with a few of his works. The buildings stand in memory of the extreme hardship endured by the German missionaries who came to the Centre to spread the gospel and "civilise the natives". The writings of some of the early pastors provide a graphic and sad insight into the brutal impact European settlement had on Aborigines in the Centre and the hardships of the missionaries whose faith must surely have been tested. Not only did they battle extremes in temperature, isolation, successive crop-destroying droughts and the scorn of pastoralists who were intent on driving off the entire Arrente Aboriginal population, but it was 11 years before they even received their first convert. The main building, now converted into a teahouse, provides some interesting displays of the life and times of the early missionaries and its most famous son.

Right: The church at Hermannsburg Historical Precinct.

The artists of Hermannsburg

Hermannsburg has long been regarded as a source for talented Aboriginal artists – Albert Namatjira its most famous.

Recognised as the first Aborigine to successfully cross the cultural and aesthetic divide from so-called "primitive symbolism" to western landscape painting, Namatjira's distinctive watercolour paintings are today hung in galleries throughout the world (In the 1950s you'd be lucky to find an Australian loungeroom that didn't have a re-production hanging on the wall).

Namatjira's life is an interesting study of a talented Aboriginal artist who painted at a time when white Australia was keen to hold up an example of the success of its policy of assimilating Aboriginal people.

While his talent is undisputed, interpretation of his work continues to provoke debate, with some suggesting its popularity was because, in western eyes, his work was the least Aboriginal. Others praise it for being innovative, yet retaining a distinctively Aboriginal form.

Hermannsburg's credentials in the art world for producing innovative Aboriginal art have extended well beyond Namatjira.

Many of its early Aboriginal artists had close historical links to Papunya, from where the Western Desert Art Movement – often recognised by its distinctive dot painting style – originated.

More recently Hermannsburg has come to celebrate The Hermannsburg Potters, a group of women who are busily transferring their art onto the surface of clay in the form of hand- made pots. Whimsical, colourful and distinctive, the art of the potters is also finding its way into galleries and households around the world. Albert would be proud.

Right: Rock Pigeons by Hermannsburg potter, Carissa Inkamala.

Mereenie Loop Road – the verdict

Authorities do not recommended you take a conventional vehicle on the Mereenie Loop Road – and it's good advice. If you're driving in a normal sedan you're likely to be a long way from home with a lot of driving ahead of you. Best to take care of your car and, hopefully, it will take care of you.

Of course, this means doubling back and a lot of extra driving,which is particularly frustrating given Kings Canyon is only about 200 kilometres from Hermannsburg or about 300 from Glen Helen, and it's all smooth sailing from there. Having said that, however, many people take the loop road regardless and if that's likely to be you, my advice is to ask beforehand about the condition of the road at Hermannsburg or Glen Helen – don't forget to get your permit – and be prepared to take you're time. Of course, if you're in a four-wheel-drive, you shouldn't have a problem.

Breakdown on the Mereenie Loop Road

I'm the sort of car mechanic who prepares for breakdowns by putting a wig and dress in the toolbox. Anything requiring more than a face-saving look beneath the bonnet and I'm marooned until help arrives.

So I figured the Gods must have decided to teach me a lesson as I sped along the Mereenie Loop Road to discover – exactly half way between Hermannsburg and Kings Canyon – that I had lost virtually an entire tank of fuel. Having pulled to a stop and taken it upon myself to at least raise the bonnet for the next car that came along, to my surprise, I discovered the problem (it was difficult to avoid as diesel was spraying in all directions). The metal join connecting the fuel line to what I assumed was the fuel pump had completely sheared away.

Well, that was enough, I thought, and with that I rolled out the fold-out chair and waited eagerly for someone with whom I would share the wisdom of my finding. Two hours passed.

Now the sun, flies, boredom and solitude have a way of coaxing you into action, I discovered, so, with no sign of life on any of the distant horizons, it occurred to me that I could use chewing gum and some electrical tape to join, and seal, the connections (didn't the Leylands try something like this?). Buoyed by my own brilliance, a full packet of gum was quickly chewed and, once applied, I set off again. That was until I was overcome with diesel fumes and pulled over to discover a trail of fuel leading from the distant hill I'd left behind towards what was now my completely empty fuel tank. Back out with the folded chair. Another two hours passed. Still nothing. Then, lo and behold, a vehicle appeared on the horizon (which I must confess was of considerable relief to me as – faced with the prospect of dying in the desert from hunger and thirst – I had immediately fallen on, and devoured, every possible ration in my car).

Snaking its way towards me was an old Holden sedan – no windscreen, crammed with Aborigines – which pulled up in a cloud of dust alongside me. "What's up, Bruddah," came the voice of my Aboriginal saviour,

barely audible over the mega-decibel din blaring from the car's radio. "Broken fuel pump," I professed proudly.

"Pommy cars, heaps of shit anyway," came the reply, and with that I thought the driver was about to resume his journey until I persisted: "Could you give me a tow to Hermannsburg, I'll gladly pay for the fuel?"

A conference between driver and passengers ensued in a language as foreign to me as car maintenance, until eventually came a voice from the back seat: "Gotta strap?"

"In the car," I replied, and with that the driver gestured me to go ahead and attach it.

Had they have watched me trying to secure the "Snatch and Grab" (that's what it said on the packet), I have no doubt my minuscule knowledge of all things mechanical would have been betrayed instantly; however, they seemed entertained enough in the car until finally I was finished. "You will drive slowly" I proffered, noting with some suspicion their obvious joviality. "Yeah, no problem," and with that we were away.

Now I'd have to say there is something a touch unsettling about being towed into a cloud of dust at about 60 kilometres an hour while watching Victorian Bitter cans being jettisoned from the car ahead of you faster than clay pigeons at an Olympic shooting tournament.

Of course, I was confident the driver was a keen student of the law, though I must confess my perception became tested as, with increasing distance, he was – I can only presume – swerving to avoid the potholes.

For me in the back, there was little more I could do but peer anxiously into my windscreen, follow the swerves, ride out the jerks and bumps and placate my anxiety by humming along to the few songs I recognised coming from the car in front.

An hour later we reached Hermannsburg with me an absolute wreck and my rescuers happy to be of assistance. I thanked them, filled their car with fuel, and waved them goodbye, vowing to burn my dress and commit to a basic mechanics course the instant I got back.

Suffice it to say, my impressions of the Mereenie Loop Road remain somewhat clouded.

"There is something a touch unsettling about being towed into a cloud of dust at about sixty kilometres an hour while watching Victorian Bitter cans being jettisoned from the car in front of you faster than clay pigeons at an Olympic shooting tournament."

Palm Valley

Sheet white, exhausted and brimming with apocalyptic warning was how I found my first fellow camper shortly after the turnoff to Palm Valley and the Finke Gorge National Park. He and his wife were coming – with considerable speed, I might add – from where I was going to and I was eager to hear about the road conditions ahead so I flagged them down. "Don't go in there," the driver blurted like a man possessed as he drew alongside me in a cloud of dust. "I've been bogged in the riverbed for three hours. Lucky to get out. Unless you've had a lot of off-road experience, I wouldn't be going any further," he warned.

"But you're in a two-wheel drive stationwagon, I'm in a four-wheel-drive Landrover," I proffered.

"The riverbed's like quicksand," he continued. "I was digging for ages. We never saw another car. I thought we were goners…"

"Did you let down your tyres?" I ventured. "Are you crazy? Then we never would have got out…" and with that their car disappeared in another cloud of dust.

* * * *

Despite this encounter, I drove on to discover Palm Valley is a top camp out and – assuming you're in a four-wheel-drive and enjoying reasonably dry conditions – a comfortable journey that combines some dramatic scenery with a bit of light, off road adventure (refer following section). It's about a 12 kilometre trip from the Hermannsburg turnoff and here's how it unfolds: The journey sees you following the Finke River – at times driving up the dry riverbed and weaving through picturesque valleys with sheer red rock walls carpeted in spinifex. The riverbed is wide; the trees in its midst, with bases covered by flotsam, providing a record of how high the Finke has risen in flood. It's hard to comprehend such a large body of water in a landscape so dry. And spare a thought for what it would be like to be caught – as some have been – camping in the riverbed and waking to a flash flood.

As you near Palm Valley, take the time to do the short Kaarranga Lookout walk from the information bay. You can't miss it. The view's great from the rocks above into the distant natural amphitheatre (right) and you can come back later if you like what you see and do the longer 5 kilometre Mpaara Track.

Further on there's a camp ground – best to secure a site early in peak season – then Cycad Gorge, appropriately named after the 300-year-old cycads that grow along the rock walls. Palm Valley, a short distance ahead, is where you're likely to find your first oasis of palms - red cabbage palms to be specific (*Livistona mariae* to be more so), hundreds of them. It's pretty impressive – according to the information bay, a botanist's paradise – boasting more than 400 plant species, many of which are rare. The cabbage palms themselves grow to 25 metres and you won't find them anywhere else in the world.

Assuming you're camping out nearby, the best time to do any of the walks is early in the morning (the earlier the better).

I can highly recommend the Mpulungkinya Track (just don't ask me how to pronounce

Right: The natural amphitheatre of Palm Valley

it) which takes in the shorter walk and sees you hopping along the riverbed and weaving through the palm clusters before ascending the valley wall and returning along the escarpment. I'd set aside three hours if you have a camera and you're keen to see some wildlife.

Some driving tips for Finke Gorge

Take a four-wheel-drive or you'll be in trouble. You have to cross the Finke River to get to Palm Valley so you're looking at some sand work and – if there's been rain – a couple of water crossings. You'll also be driving across rocks so there will be some "walking the car" and tossing of passengers, particularly in the last 3 kilometres (having said that, however, I never found a need to drop into low gear). A good rule of thumb if this is your first time off the bitumen is to stick to the other car tracks and maintain your speed in the sand. If you're unsure of a crossing, grab some shade and wait for a more experienced driver to go first. Take some comfort knowing the route is popular and it's well patronised by tour operators so you won't be alone for long in the unlikely event you get into trouble. There's also a resident ranger in the park during the tourist season.

Above: The palm clustered gorges of Palm Valley.
Right: The magnificent Wedge Tailed Eagle. Remember, they are heavy birds and cannot fly off quickly so if you see one on the road ahead of you, slow down

Kings Canyon

Watarrka

"The country round its foot is by far the best I have seen in this region; could it be transported to any civilised land its springs, glens, gorges, ferns, Zamias and flowers would charm the eyes and hearts of toil-worn men who are condemned to live and die in crowded towns."

– Ernest Giles, 1873

Such praise from one of Australia's most eloquent 19th century explorers stands as the earliest testament to the appeal of Kings Canyon, long regarded as the jewel of the Centre's George Gill Range.

And the good news is that more than 150 years later, much of what Giles wrote about can still be seen today – panoramic views from the top of the range, sheer 100 metre canyon walls, lush spring-fed waterholes shaded by prehistoric palms and dramatic sandstone shapes sculptured into the landscape over millions of years.

In short, it's special – in my opinion, one of the best gorge walks in Australia (there must

Left: The spectacular view through the gorge from the Garden of Eden. **Right:** The palm-fringed waters of Kings Canyon.

Kings Canyon Rim Walk at a glance

TIME: Allow 3 – 4 hours

BEST TIME OF YEAR: All year round.

GRADE: Tough for the ascent (just take it easy, it's well worth it). After that it's all downhill.

HIGHLIGHT: The views from the edge of the canyon walls.

NEED TO TAKE: A hat, good shoes, something to drink, a snack and plenty of film.

START: The climb carpark.

FINISH: As above.

be some reason why I dragged by bung knee and blistered feet up and down the gorge three times in 24 hours). There are two walks into Kings Canyon – The Creek Walk, which takes you about a kilometre into the Canyon along its basin, or the 6 kilometre Rim Walk, both of which begin from the national park interpretive shelter.

Kings Canyon Rim Walk

For the Rim Walk it needs to be said that – as with most experiences of worth – you need to earn it, and the bad news is that you can expect to advance your pound of flesh during the first 15 minutes or so as you ascend the 150 metres to the top of the gorge. It's an effort (by my calculation, about 500 steep steps and 30 fly swats), but the experience on top makes it all well worth it. Wander through the so-called Lost City – a labyrinth of giant sandstone blocks weathered into domes, scramble over

the blistered rock trails, goad yourself to the edge of the chasm and peer deep down into the valley below. It's great, though I can assure you the view at the edge is not for the faint-hearted.

About an hour into the walk you descend several flights of wooden stairs to a boardwalk suspended over the lush valley floor. From there you can deviate about 10 minutes each way following the palm-fringed base of ridge to the Valley of Eden where there's a large rock pool (the rangers prefer people don't swim in it as it's the only source of water for the resident wildlife). Just around the corner lies a stunning view of the entire valley bordered on one side by the arched wall of the canyon.

Once you return to the stairs and climb the opposite wall to the escarpment, you can again wander the rim, looking back on where you were earlier. It's a dramatic sheer face of ochre hues – fantastic to catch at sunset when the late afternoon shadows accentuate the edges of the gorge. Wander along the rim until the sun has virtually disappeared, then descend a gradual, stepped slope, arriving back to the interpretive centre around dark. One thing I can guarantee, you'll sleep well that night.

- Make sure you veer right at the Lookout Walk sign with the lizard on it, or you'll miss some of the best views.
- If you go as far as the Garden of Eden, clamber (carefully) around the corner for one of the best views of the valley.
- Plan to arrive at the carpark by three o'clock. The day will be cooling and by the time you're on top, the setting sun will be illuminating the gorge walls.
- Take a drink and a sandwich to sit and enjoy the views.

Above: Jumping on the domes of The Lost City.
Right: Looking down on to Kings Creek.

Kings Canyon which way up?

Because the Kings Canyon Rim Walk starts and finishes at the same place, there are two options for making the ascent – clockwise, which is recommended by National Parks, or anticlockwise which can prove a temptation given it appears to promise the less strenuous ascent. While I like to get the hard stuff out of the way as quickly as possible, I can understand people opting for a gentler ascent, but, I'd have to say, it simply doesn't make sense. As many appeared to go anti-clockwise while I was there, I thought I'd provide some food for thought for when you're standing at the crossroads.

- By going clockwise, you've got the hard work out of the way while you're refreshed and you can enjoy the rest of the walk knowing the worst is behind you.

- With the clockwise walk, your ascent is over once you've climbed 150 metres. By going the other way, you're climbing – though more gradually – for about a kilometre – and you still won't have seen the canyon.

- Clockwise is safer. You're a lot more likely to be fatigued at the end of the walk, which is when you would have to make the demanding, steeper descent.

- Coming down the steep side is more jarring on your legs and joints.

- If everyone travels in the same direction (clockwise), you're not having to walk around people, which not only makes the journey more enjoyable and safer, it minimises erosion.

Of course, having pointed this out, there may well be a logical reason why so many people I saw were going the opposite way, and I did ask a few people -- but most were too out of breath to even reply.

THE CREEK WALK

While wandering the rim provides the most spectacular views of Kings Canyon, the short Creek Walk into the canyon's basin offers a less demanding, tranquil experience. Looking up beyond the pale limbs of the majestic ghost gums, the canyon's orange cliff face lights up with the early morning light. It's a serene setting, particularly when the cool air caresses the valley and rustles the leaves overhead. The songs of birds and the gurgling of the creek lend themselves to – as two women along the trail demonstrated while I was there – perching on a boulder and reading a good book.

Left: Looking up into the cliffs of Kings Canyon from the Creek Walk.

"Most people come to Australia hoping to do three things — to climb the Rock, to swim in the Great Barrier Reef and to talk to a blackfella".

- Keith Aitkien, tour guide

After a couple of weeks in Central Australia, it's difficult not to accumulate questions about the Aboriginal culture which go beyond the books, the brochures and the politically correct interpretative plaques. When it's all said and done, you can't help thinking wouldn't it be great to simply sit down and just have a conversation with an Aboriginal person...

You only have to read the Lilla Tours comments book to realise that Keith Aitkien presents a refreshingly candid and much-welcomed view of the Aboriginal culture in Central Australia. Born to a full-blood Aboriginal mother and a white father, Keith's perspective comes from having, as he says, "a foot in both camps".

"To a white man I'll always be black, and to a blackfella I'll always be white but I accept that and I try to share some of what I have learned with both cultures," he says.

The Lilla Cultural Tour begins about 9 kilometres from the Kings Canyon turnoff at a large rustic bush shelter made of desert oak beams, hessian walls and a spinifex roof dripping with hardened ochre. Keith starts his talk there before everyone heads off on a short walk which takes in nearby Aboriginal sacred sites, rock paintings and waterholes.

While the stories Keith tells provide a valuable insight into the Aboriginal culture of the surrounding region, what makes his tour exceptional is his simple interpretation of seemingly complex Aboriginal subjects and his willingness — and ability — to answer the prickly questions about Aboriginal people which are on everyone's mind. While he tells you stories of his people and familiarises you with the surrounding land, he invites questions about his culture and provides thoughtful answers. To an interested and eager audience, his casual manner quickly opens the door to talk of politics, racism, drinking, government dependency, even sexual practices. "Of course, some things are sacred and private but I like to think I can answer anyone's questions. I realise there's a lot about the Aboriginal culture people don't understand so I try and open their eyes – at least a little – to what my people can see and what is important to us."

At one point Keith describes the bush surrounding him as a giant supermarket ("only it doesn't have the freezers and check outs"). "This land looks after us like a mother, providing us with food, shelter and water. We are its children. To us its features read like a book – a bible if you like – with stories of wisdom which have been passed on to us over many generations."

At an overhanging cave painted with symbols, Keith unravels some of the mystique surrounding Aboriginal art

Right: Keith Aitkien sits prepared to share his refreshing perspective with the world.

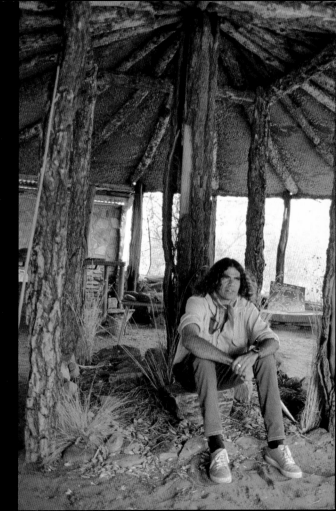

by sitting and smoothing the surface of the sand in front of him. With his fingers, he gently draws concentric circles on the ground and crescents, traditionally representing waterholes and camp sites. But then he alters them to represent what he says is a pool party and champagne glasses. He draws straight lines arriving at the concentric circles which represent the path people have taken to get to the party, then he draws wiggly lines coming out of the circles, representing their departure. The pattern and symbols all look very familiar. "This story carries a message which is important to both your culture and mine," he says, adding with a laugh "It means don't drink and drive."... But this is merely the story of this drawing he emphasises, ensuring that what he has done has not diminished the value of Aboriginal art, but simply made it easier for us to understand how painting is used to communicate among the Aboriginal people.

The two hours with Keith pass quickly providing a valuable insight into Aboriginal culture for a group obviously eager to learn more.

If you've climbed Kings Canyon and you have a bit of time to spare, I highly recommend his tour.

Right: A late afternoon light falls on the Giles Range.

ULURU
Ayers Rock

U l u r u
An introduction

Uluru surpasses all the superlatives which have been bestowed upon it. It's a magnificent natural feature of profound spiritual significance to the Aboriginal people – truly worthy of its World Heritage status. Few who have stood at its base could fail to be moved by its sense of presence and timeless majesty. Witness its changing moods at sunrise or sunset and the Rock will enchant you – as it has the many who have come before you, and the millions who are likely to follow.

According to the Anangu Aborigines, who are recognised as its traditional custodians, Uluru is part of what they call Tjukurpa – a complex belief system which governs their daily lives today as it has done since time immemorial. To the Anangu, the Tjukurpa is their religion – a spiritual framework and a philosophy for day-to-day living directly handed down to them by their ancient ancestors – supernatural beings who roamed the earth's surface and created the natural features we see today. It was these beings who created the laws by which the Anangu live and inscribed the customs of their culture which govern their traditional behaviour, tell them how they came to be and direct the deep affinity they have for their land. The Tjukurpa is perpetually replenished through the stories and songs sung by the Anangu today.

Left: Uluru at sunrise

103

The walks at a glance

The Circuit Walk (9.2 km/3–4 hours).
Grading: Easy. **Features**: An intimate experience of Uluṟu. (Takes in Mutitjulu and Mala Walks)
Tip: If you do it without a guide, get the self-guided tour booklet from the Cultural Centre.

The Mutitjulu Walk (1 km/45 minutes).
Grading: Easy. **Features**: Waterhole, rock art and story about "scars" on Uluṟu created during the mythological battle between two ancestral snakes.

The Climb (1.6 km/2–3 hours).
Features: The view. **Grading**: Hard. **The Consequence**: You will offend some Anangu Aborigines.

The Mala Walk (2 km/90 minutes).
Grading: Easy. **Features**: Cave art, stories and waterhole (Free Guided tours are conducted daily).

The Liru Walk (2 km/45 minutes one way)
Grading: Easy. **Features**: Interpretation by Anangu guide.

To understand Uluṟu in context of the Tjukurpa, it needs to be understood that there is not one single story of its creation. Uluṟu is the subject of many stories of Aboriginal mythology which are intricately interwoven into their deep and complex belief system. It also needs to be recognised that many of the stories are sacred to the Anangu and can only be revealed to those who have been initiated through time-honoured rites of passage.

Regardless, since Uluṟu was first opened to tourism, authorities have struggled to give visitors an interpretation of Uluṟu that would satisfy their fleeting curiosity in a way that makes sense to them. Hence various stories were created, and terms like the Brain, the Hat, the Kangaroo Tail and the Organ Cave passed through various phases of palatability until finally they were all rejected by an audience now receptive to referring to Uluṟu's features by their Aboriginal name, and hearing stories about Uluṟu faithfully recounted by Aboriginal people.

European history

"...This rock is certainly the most wonderful natural feature I have ever seen."

- William Gosse, 1873.

And so were recorded the words of Uluru's first "tourist" – William Christie Gosse, not the first man to lay eyes on the Rock, but certainly the first European to lay a foot on it (he climbed it and named it Ayers Rock after Sir Henry Ayers, who was then Chief Secretary for South Australia).

While Gosse won the accolades and was recorded for his deed in all the history books, it was actually Ernest Giles who was the first European to sight the rock a year earlier but had more pressing matters and moved on.

Until 1920, pastoral leases were extended across most of Central Australia. Ayers Rock and Mt Olga then became part of a reserve set aside for Aboriginal people until 1958 when the area was declared a national park. Aboriginal Land Rights were declared in 1976 then, in 1985 – after a long struggle – the title deeds of the national park which included its two most prominent features, Uluru and Kata Tjuta were officially handed back to the Anangu Aborigines.

The park was subsequently leased to the federal government for 99 years and has since been World Heritage listed.

The Geology

Geologists have a somewhat dry explanation for how Uluru came to be. Made from a coarse, grained sandstone called Arkos, the giant rock, which rises 348 metres above the desert, was once part of a sea bed known as the Amadeus Basin until massive underground forces squeezed and buckled the land, causing what is now Uluru to rise in an almost vertical formation. Over 300 million years, the sea disappeared and wind, rain and extremes in temperatures have worn away the edges leaving the scored surface of the rock and what we see today.

Two thirds of the rock is believed to be under the sand. It is 3.6 kilometres in length and 2.4 kilometres wide, with a 9.4 kilometres circumference on the ground.

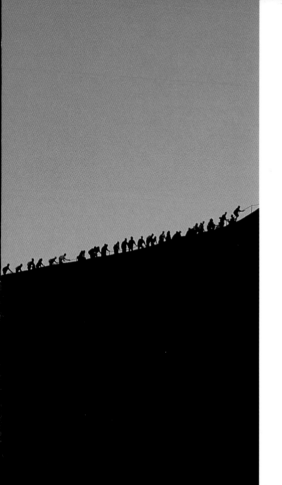

To climb or not to climb

Like many visitors, I arrived at Uluṟu undecided on whether or not I'd climb the Rock.

On one hand, I'd read of how Uluṟu is revered as a sacred site and that climbing it would be offensive to its Aboriginal custodians. On the other, I'd heard that the traditional Aboriginal custodians – "if they even exist" – really don't care if it's scaled or not. And then, of course, there was my own reluctance to pass up the chance to do the testosterone thing and stand on top of one of the world's most recognised landmarks.

So, torn between conscience and desire, I arrived at the base of Uluṟu where I agonisingly resolved to postpone my ascent – at least until I'd gathered a bit more information on the subject.

The first thing I discovered was that the climbing of Uluṟu is a prickly issue. Parks Australia, the federal agency which joint manages the park, doesn't encourage the climb.

Left: Aboriginal people call the climbers "Minga" because they look like ants climbing. Not a bad description methinks.

Administratively and financially it's a burden having to constantly rescue people suffering from exhaustion and sprained limbs (they rescue as many as 15 people a month during the peak tourist season and more than 30 people have been killed making the climb. It also points out the climbing of Uluru has become an environmental issue due to the physical impact thousands of climbers are having on the rock. And then, of course, there's the position it takes on behalf of its Aboriginal partners (more on that later). In summary, Parks Australia holds the view that Uluru should be viewed to be experienced – not walked over.

The tourism industry weighs in, having fought vigorously to have the climb kept open. A report was commissioned by Central Australian tourism operators showing that if the climb was closed, visitor numbers to the Centre would fall significantly. Politicians and key decision makers have been actively lobbied.

It's also argued that nearby Aboriginal communities, for which Uluru has become a substantial cash cow, would also feel the pinch if the climb were closed.

Cafe and bar talk around Alice Springs provides an interesting, if not contentious, insight into the debate. "Uluru was never a sacred site to Aborigines until there was a dollar to be made. There aren't any traditional landowners. Even the name Uluru is a joke. It's a generic name for large round rock – nothing special. All the do-gooders gathered up distant tribes from around the county to hand the rock back to and needed an Aboriginal name for the handover, so they stumbled across Uluru and said, yeah, that will do (Uluru, or Ayers Rock as it was called after European settlement, was symbolically handed back to the Aborigines by the federal government in 1985). Just recently, a prominent Aboriginal came out publicly saying the real traditional custodians have never actually been asked whether they care if people climb the rock or not."

Perhaps the most persuasive side of the argument belongs to Uluru's local Aborigines, whose views are represented in the park's cultural centre and transmitted through a range of collateral handed out to visitors (remarkably, many of them receive it after they have completed the climb, as the cultural centre is the second port of call).

Through photos, interactive audio presentations and video tapes, those recognised as being Uluru's traditional custodians ask visitors not to climb Uluru. Simply stated, they say, "We would prefer you do not climb the rock." Their request gains more momentum as visitors are informed that Uluru was, and still is, a sacred site, that the actual climb was once strictly reserved for rites of passage under ancient Aboriginal law and that, as Uluru's traditional custodians, Aborigines are genuinely grieved when mishaps or deaths occur to climbers on the Rock. In a bid to relate the climb to something non-Aboriginal people may understand, articulate spokespeople say the thousands of tourists clambering over Uluru are as offensive to some Aborigines as thousands of tourists traipsing over a family grave or scaling St Paul's Cathedral.

So, dear reader, this is what I have been able to divine with a few questions and a bit of reading and I thought I'd pass it on as, quite obviously, the decision on whether to climb Uluru continues to present a dilemma for many.

Personally, I think that for as long as the climb remains open and people arrive with the expectation they can climb, the decision to take to the rail should be a personal one.

Hopefully, the views I've passed on here will at least contribute to visitors making a more informed decision.

As for me, I returned to the base of Uluru where a climber shared with me what was obviously a popular reason for making the ascent. "Absolutely fantastic," he said. "Y'know, I wasn't sure whether I'd climb it or not because of all that Aboriginal stuff but in the end I figured that if the Aborigines really didn't want us to climb Uluru they would have just told us not to."

… It was a valid point and I can only surmise why they apparently haven't.

Regardless, for what it's worth, I decided not to climb Uluru as it became obvious to me that it is offensive to at least some traditional Aboriginal people. I'm also of the view there is far more to be gained from the experience of visiting Uluru by choosing not to do the climb.

"I've come from halfway around the world just to climb this rock."

"If the Aborigines didn't want us to climb the rock they simply should have said so."

"Cultural interpretation aside, Uluru is a beautiful natural feature. Why would people want to deface it by climbing on it?"

"Uluru is sacred. We would prefer you don't climb the Rock."

"For as long as it remains open, people will continue to climb the Rock."

- Some random comments

Wandering Uluru

"There's a lot more to be learned at the base of Uluru than there is by climbing to the top."
– Anangu guide

My guided tour of the Liru Walk started at eight O'clock with "Joe", our guide, passing out a few props – two spears, one for hunting another for ceremonial punishment, a digging stick, a wooden bowl which the women use to collect food and a womera, or throwing stick. In his dilly bag he also carried a belt made from human hair – "This is all my ancestors used to wear before clothes" – and a ring made of spinifex and feathers which the women use to carry the bowls on their heads.

It's a casual and informative walk, with Uluru providing a spectacular backdrop as Joe refers to the plants we see by their Aboriginal names and tells us stories of their medicinal purposes. "This small purple flower provides moisture for our throat during long journeys without water," he says. In between inviting and answering questions about his culture, Joe stops at a small shelter and makes a fire before showing us how to make the glue from spinifex which is used to repair traditional implements. He explains the men's tools: the belt made from hair, the hunting spear with the barb designed so the wounded kangaroo drags it if he survives to show the hunters where he's gone, the ceremonial spear which is used for punishment (one

thrust of that through your thigh and you'll be back on the straight-and-narrow, I can assure you). He empties the women's gathering bowl and tries to balance it on his head, inviting guests to do the same. "Part of getting in touch with my feminine side," he says. There were stories of symbols carved into the ground that related to Uluṟu and of the battle with the mythical serpent, Lira which left the rock scarred. We hear of the Aboriginal people's deep affinity for their land; how as a people they never take any more than is needed. Still walking, we pause and – as if sensing our earlier disappointment that a lighter was used to ignite the first fire – Joe used his spear thrower, a piece of wood, rabbit droppings and some grass to ignite another.

Finally the tour ended up at the base of Uluṟu directly in front of the climb, where one of the visitors asked Joe a question I think we'd all been keen to hear answered. "What do I think about the climb?" said Joe rhetorically. "I reckon it will be closed in another 10 years."

And we were all happy to leave it at that.

The Base Walk

In my opinion, wandering the 9 kilometre track that circles the base of Uluṟu is the best way to experience the Rock. While I'd recommend doing at least one of the shorter Liru, Mala or Mutitjulu walks – ideally with an Anangu guide – the Base Walk gives you a more intimate appreciation of Uluṟu as both a spiritual and natural feature. A tip before you start, though: Drop in to the cultural centre and get a copy of the Mutitjulu and Mala Walks booklet, which provides a cultural insight into some of what you'll be looking at, otherwise, you'll need to be satisfied with the information panels at some of the points of interest.

The walk around the base of Uluṟu is a casual way of experiencing the Rock (if you've come in your own car, it's certainly safer than driving into oncoming traffic every time a feature of Uluṟu grabs your attention). Wandering casually along its base in the early or late afternoon light, you can take your time to appreciate the scale and grandeur of Uluṟu as a natural sculpture, honed over the millennia by the forces of nature. At close quarters, you can study the undulating curves of its surface – sensual, if the light is right – the varying textures, the contrasts of colour – shades of brown and red, set against the stark blue sky. Standing in its shadow and looking up, it's hard not to be in awe of its size, the sheer walls of rock that dwarf nearby trees. And the experience is likely to reward you with some appreciation of how the stories of Uluru's features came to be. It's hard not to look at the "gashes" on the side of the rock and not imagine the wounds resulting from a mighty mythological battle; it's satisfying to recognise impressions or shapes in the rock and associate them with symbols and stories you may have heard of the Tjukurpa. Walking past sections of Uluru which are sacred to the Anangu and still used today for ancient ceremonies, it is so much easier to feel and accept the significance of Uluru to Aboriginal people.

As you will see on the walk, there is much that cannot be photographed, features which are now destined never to be seen by people unless they actually come here. The honeycombed side of Uluru, the caves, the waterholes – all become subjects of fascination.

All up, the Base Walk will take you 3–4 hours and if there is anything of particular significance you can always come back later or find out a bit more about it at the Cultural Centre.

I, for one, was completely entertained for the entire walk.

Great expectations

It seems that everyone you talk to who has been to Uluru remembers a time when there were fewer restrictions: "We could wander wherever we wanted; stand in solitude to witness the changing colours, camp out in the desert and wake up to Uluru at dawn." Nowadays, of course, that's all changed. The Rock is cordoned off apart from two thin walking trails around its base, several large sunset and sunrise viewing areas for cars and coaches, and the climb. No visitors in the park just after sunset; gates open just before sunrise. Yellow lines determine where you can or can't stop in your car, shin-high barrier wires prevent you going where you shouldn't – and so it goes on.

Standing amid the crowd at one of the designated viewing areas at sunset or sunrise, visitors could be forgiven for thinking the Uluru experience is far removed from that of the not-so-distant past and that it's become over-regulated. But it needs to be remembered that back then – and we're talking less than 10 years ago – there was never 450000 tourists a year clamouring for a photograph and Uluru was yet to enjoy its status as an international tourist icon. Roads were never as good, buses and planes were never as frequent and accommodation was not so sophisticated.

The management of Uluru – as with any world-class natural attraction – is a delicate balance between preservation and access. It's an ongoing challenge for authorities and the public. Greater restrictions are an unfortunate, though inevitable, by-product of a more widely circulating population eager to see the world.

But spare a thought for what tourism will be in a century's time. Will access to our most spectacular and sensitive sites become an experience for the privileged few – less people paying a small fortune to get in? How much of the experience in the future will be virtual and how much of it will be real – will we spend two hours in the cultural centre and be allowed just 10 minutes on site? How far ahead will you have to plan for your holiday – will we have to book ahead for our children? It's food for thought ... and, if nothing else, maybe something to distract you while you're anxiously queuing to get through the entrance gate at Uluru in time for sunrise.

Right: Uluru after the rain.

Recommended reading

Regardless of whether Bill Harney's interpretation of the spiritual significance of Uluru and its features is accurate or not, his book – To Ayers Rock and Beyond – remains a fascinating record of his tenure as the first park ranger at Uluru from 1957 to 1962.

Quite obviously, the author has an empathy and deep respect for the Aboriginal people and their culture; his intent was to record his observations and provide a rare insight into Uluru, and the people – black and white – who journeyed to see it.

The book is easily read. It's both entertaining and insightful and – in this humble writer's opinion – compulsive reading for anyone looking for a richer insight into Uluru:

" I had learned from working with Aborigines all over the Northern Territory that impatient questions would only bring on vague answers. The true tribesman has learned from experience of white people that many questioners are happy to get the answers they desire."

The sunrise procession

Every morning about an hour before sunrise, hundreds of tourists rush from their hotel rooms and tents into the darkness to make their way to the edge of Uluru so they can photograph the ancient leviathan stir in the early morning light. It's an entertaining ritual – if you like, a crowd warmer to the main event – which begins when you enter a stream of glowing red tail-lights meandering from Yulara through the national park towards the designated photography site on the eastern side of Uluru. For the eager new arrivals the journey can be traumatic. There's the agonisingly slow nudging towards the park entrance gate (why is it always the car in front that doesn't have the right change?), followed by the depressing recognition that with all the people ahead, you're probably already too late to get a good position. Faced with the prospect of arriving after it's all over, you consider speeding, but overtaking's out of the question as everyone ahead is running bumper to bumper and invariably the one you overtake and run off the road will be the one who pulls up alongside you at the viewing site. It's a long 20 kilometre journey, but the anxiety is unfounded as you're likely to arrive with time to spare.

The sunrise crowd at Uluru is a spectacle in itself. Set between the dark, imposing form of Uluru and the soft pastel colours emerging from the distant horizon lies what appears to be a never-ending corridor of cars and two-storey buses (someone counted 47 buses on the day I was there). Milling around them are hundreds of tourists chatting excitedly, eagerly waiting for the dawn light to deliver that much-promised photograph of Uluru aglow. The more organised have prepared for the cool desert morning (it can drop to less than zero) and have arrived early to sit peering out of cars parked at prime positions. There are clusters of Japanese squatting on fold-out chairs sipping hot drinks; those standing close to the barrier are rigidly defending their positions.

As dawn begins to break, the anticipation is palpable until the first rays of sunlight fall on Uluru, triggering an explosion of artificial light. This goes on for about 10 minutes. Then – as if a silent command is given, everyone ceases and gets back into their cars or onto the buses then disappears, leaving you standing alone.

In contrast, the mood of the sunset viewing site is more casual and intimate. The coach crowd has been designated a separate area and many of the viewers are more patient, having spent most of the day wandering around Uluru. Typically, the Germans will have taken up prime positions at the viewing barrier well ahead of the rest and will be sitting smugly as the other arrivals file in. Couples also arrive well in advance and set up tables and chairs with food and drink. Linked by common experience, conversations are started with strangers in neighbouring parking lots. Ample time is taken to bask in the glow of Uluru and enjoy the moment well before, and long after, the sun has set.

ROCK ART

Didgeridoos would have to be the most popular souvenir item requested by visitors at the Maruku Arts and Craft Centre at Uluṟu, which presents a bit of a problem really, as they don't have any – but there's a good reason.

Didgeridoos – popular souvenirs and excellent musical instruments though they are – have nothing to do with Aborigines from Central Australia. Traditionally, they are made and used by Aborigines in northern Australia, so, if you're looking to buy a didgeridoo while you're visiting Uluṟu – or anywhere else in the Centre for that matter – bear in mind, you're likely to be purchasing an imported product.

On the other hand, if you want to buy some art or craft that has originated from the Aboriginal communities surrounding Uluṟu – and you like wood – you've come to the right place.

The Maruku Arts and Craft Centre, located at the Cultural Centre at Uluṟu, represents the work of more than 800 Aboriginal artists from 19 communities surrounding Uluṟu.

Each month, employees jump into their truck and wander

Right: Walter Pukutiwara - one of the founders of the Maruku Art and Craft Centre.

the region collecting the art from remote desert communities.

What makes the work of the Anangu Aborigines distinctive is that their medium is wood, most of their designs are carved onto traditional implements and weapons such as boomerangs, spears, throwing sticks and wira (food or water carriers), and that many of the patterns and symbols used in their decorations are drawn from the Tjukurpa – the Creation story of the Anangu people.

Like most art, the wood carving of the Anangu artists is evolving, and a tool or weapon which was once made purely for functional purposes has now become an important medium for artistic expression.

As with the conversion from sand painting to acrylic on canvas (dot paintings), the Anangu have adapted their art by applying thin pieces of red-hot wire to wood, much of which is still drawn from the roots and trunks of trees by traditional means.

While no single person or influence has been accredited with introducing the process, it is thought to have originated around the 1950s, and may have started with fencing wire heated in ashes and used for branding

Regardless, today the medium provides an exciting vehicle for many local artists, some of whom have gone on to use the technique to create whimsical sculptures of snakes and lizards, important characters from their ancient stories.

Of course, the craft may not sound as good as a didgeridoo, but one thing is likely – it's sure to have come from the Centre.

Right: The Maruku Art and Craft Centre.

Climbing (over) Uluru

I like helicopters; they are effortless and provide a perspective you can only imagine on the ground. Duck under the rotors (I can't help it), don the headset, struggle with the seatbelt, sit around while the pilot does his pre-flight check and... lift off. The whirring blades, the tilt, the surge forward, the rushing air. Then just sit back and watch the vast expanse of Australia's inland desert unfold beneath you.

Flying over Yulara you edge your way excitedly towards Uluru, with Kata Tjuta sitting tantalisingly in the distance. While the view is reward enough, added to it is the satisfaction of knowing you are seeing one of the world's great icons as only few others have.

Top Tip: Take the flight late afternoon as the setting sun paints the sky a deep mauve and inflames the tops of Uluru and Kata Tjuta. Absolutely magic.

Sounds of silence

There's another experience which I couldn't pass up while I was visiting Uluru – the Sounds of Silence dinner in the desert, put on by Ayers Rock Resort. It's not cheap, but it's special; here's why.

The evening begins when you are picked up and taken on a short trip into the desert where you alight and wander to the top of a nearby sand dune. There, waiters in crisply pressed uniforms greet you with a glass of chilled champagne and circulate with trays of exotic Australian canapé's while you mingle with the other guests. In the background, a lone didgeridoo player sets the mood. In the distance, clearly visible from where you're standing, you can see Uluru and Kata Tjuta beginning to glow in the dwindling afternoon light.

It's a rare audience, standing, just watching, occasionally moved to whispers of awe, as the colours of Uluru and Kata Tjuta move from ochre to red to a dark mauve and eventually into darkness. By then, you've been invited to be seated at nearby tables. The setting is romantic – white table cloths

Left: Poolside at Ayers Rock Resort

and plates with silver settings, candles, uniformed waiters standing by while chefs add the final touches to the meal you're about to enjoy ... all – most remarkably – set in the middle of the Australian desert.

Once you're seated, wines are served and guests select from a menu of succulent Australian fare. There's an opportunity to sample kangaroo and crocodile; for the less adventurous, there are barramundi, minted lamb, seasoned beef and vegetables. Amid the tinkle of cutlery, a toast is proposed and a poem is read before all the lights are extinguished and guests are invited to listen to the sounds of the Australian desert.

Silence. Several minutes pass.

Then a modulated, well-educated voice breaks the silence and a powerful sword of light slices through the darkness from the hand of an astronomer to rest on a distant constellation. "The star Betelgeuse, 300 times the size of our own sun, marks the shoulder of Orion. Capricorn here, Aries over there, if you're a Virgo, this is you here." For the next half-hour, modern astrology and Aboriginal mythology are combined as a spellbound audience is taken on a tour of the heavens. Desserts and ports are served later; guests politely excuse themselves from conversations to peer through the astronomer's giant telescopes ... until, all too soon, the transport arrives and we are spirited back to recall and savour what must be an exceptional experience.

Big Tip: Book early.

Above: Dawn at Uluṟu **Right:** Kata Tjuṯa

> *"Mt Olga is the more wonderful and grotesque, Mount Ayers is the more ancient and sublime."*
>
> – Ernest Giles, 1873

It's a sad fact that many visitors to the Centre simply don't get to spend much time at Kata Tjuṯa.

With the average visitor spending just 1.8 days at Yulara – most of whom are on a mission to see the colours of Uluṟu or experience any one of a number of tours designed around it – Kata Tjuṯa tends to receive just a quick visit.

Which means – and here's the tip – there's a lot fewer people there, particularly after the coaches have all raced back to catch the sunset on Uluṟu.

Now I need to make a confession here: while I like to make a point of doing most walks, regrettably, I didn't do the 3 hour, 7.4 kilometre Valley of the Winds walk into the

Right: Kata Tjuta

formation. I'd wandered the base of Uluru the day before to discover my ill-fitting shoes had left blisters on the bottom of my feet the size of pillows. Hence, I had to be satisfied with the one-hour Walpa or Olga Gorge Walk and taking photographs of Kata Tjuta from a distance (of course, with the opportunity missed, all I've done is read about how fantastic it is – great views from lookout points, dwarfed by towering domes, deep significance as a sacred men's place etc, etc.)

However, I did manage to get some reasonable photographs and can highly recommend standing on the western side of Kata Tjuta at sunset (or the eastern side at sunrise). While not commanding the same physical presence as Uluru, you have a lot more room to "play" and you are likely to have a lot less people in your way.

The formation of Kata Tjuta (meaning many heads) covers about 35 square kilometres. It's about 53 kilometres from Yulara. It's highest point is the top of Mt Olga at 546metres which is 200 metres higher than Uluru.

I'd recommend at least a full day trip at Kata Tjuta (and that you wear good shoes the day before).

Above and left: Kata Tjuṯa .

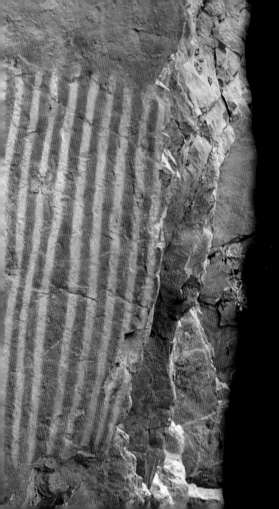

The east MacDonnell Ranges

Introduction to
"The East Macs"

The eastern side of the MacDonnell Ranges is less popular than the west, mainly because visitors, pressed for time, often have to make a choice between the two. As a result, the distinct appeal of the eastern side of the ranges, despite its gorges, Aboriginal art and fascinating early history, tends to comes in second and often gets overlooked. Of course, this is good news for travellers with more time who want to avoid the crowds.

Shortly out of Alice, along the Ross River Highway, are **Emily and Jessie Gaps**, which are both pleasant breaks, though nothing to write home about. According to local Aborigines, the two sites are part of the Caterpillar Dreaming trail. A wander through the small waterhole at Emily Gap will see you standing in front of some distinctive rock art (previous page). From there it's on to **Corroboree Rock** (pictured left) which, apparently, has nothing to do with dancing but was once used to store sacred Aboriginal objects. The sealed road leads to its base and, after a short walk around, you're on the road again, heading for **Trephina Gorge Nature Park**. Trephina Gorge is a pleasant overnight camping spot with sheer cliffs and watercourses lined with River Red Gums. Because it receives fewer travellers, you're likely to see more wildlife – birds and rock wallabies – particularly on an early morning walk. I can recommend the one-hour Trephina Gorge Walk overlooking the gorge, and the one-hour Panorama Walk which affords excellent views over the surrounding terrain, particularly if you set off shortly after first light. Thinking better of the full-day Ridgetop Walk, I settled for the John Hayes Rockhole and a swim which was at the end of

Left: Corroboree Rock.

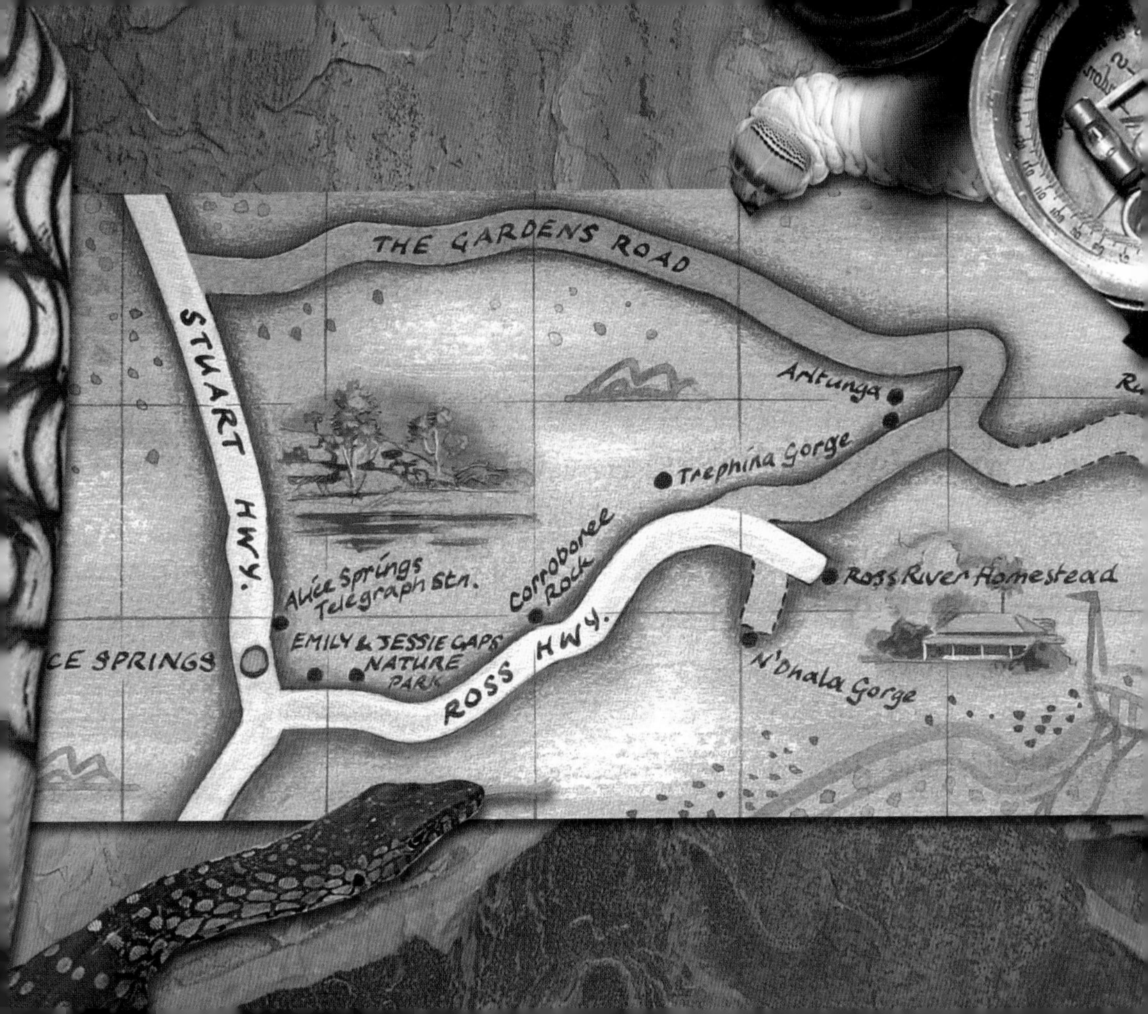

THE GARDENS ROAD
STUART HWY.
Arltunga
Trephina Gorge
Corroboree Rock
Alice Springs Telegraph Stn.
Ross River Homestead
EMILY & JESSIE GAPS NATURE PARK
CE SPRINGS
ROSS HWY.
N'Dhala Gorge

a short four-wheel drive track. Shortly after Trephina and heading east you'll need to make a decision on whether to go to Ross River Homestead, which marks the end of the highway, or to deviate about 30 kilometres along the unsealed road to Arltunga and beyond. **Ross River Homestead** is a relaxing stopover with meals and accommodation, horse and camel rides. If you want to get away a bit and see some Aboriginal petroglyphs, a four-wheel-drive will take you on to **N'Dhala Gorge Nature Park** where some poor soul (you'll know what I mean when you try and identify them) has apparently counted 6000 separate engravings. If Arltunga is where you're headed, you would have had to turn off about 7 kilometres back along the highway.

Left: Trephina Gorge. Top: Curious rock wallaby in Trephina Gorge. Right: View from Panorama Walk, Trephina Gorge

Photographer's tips

Photography, according to all the visitor surveys, is by far the most popular activity for people visiting the Centre so I thought I'd round up a few tips which might help (suffice it to say, I also have a few rolls of film which will never see the light of day).

On photographing Uluru:

It's Uluru that decides whether or not you get "that" photo of the Rock. If the conditions aren't perfect – and I'm told by coach drivers it is rare, maybe eight times a year – you simply won't get that almost surreal red you see on postcards. You need cloud, reflection and the sunlight at just the right angle (so don't be disappointed if your shot rates only a 9/10).

• If you are carrying a polarising filter, use it sparingly as it tends to over-darken the skies.

On photographing the Centre in general:

• Once you have taken the photo you think has successfully recorded the scene you want to remember, look for an angle which will interpret it differently – move in and out, stoop down or climb etc, etc.

• Add different layers to your photograph. First clearly identify the subject, then look for features – people or objects – you can add to the middle distance and foreground to enhance the photo. Having said that, make sure the process doesn't detract from the subject.

• Scan souvenir books and travel magazines to get different ideas (I've always said I'm not an original thinker, just a tasteful thief).

• If you're lucky, there are six minutes of perfect light a day – that's three minutes early morning and three minutes late afternoon. As often as possible, plan your day to be in position for both.

• I'm not a purist; filters are fun and give more scope to your photographs, particularly if weather is bad or light is extreme. I carry yellow, warm, neutral density filters as well as graduated mauve and tobacco filters, plus the polariser.

• Remember: film will be the cheapest part of your holiday so bring more than you think you will need.

• Wherever possible use a tripod. It's a lot more effort but the images tend to be a lot sharper.

• I generally prefer a slow, 50 ASA transparency film (I'm a Velvia man) for greater quality and colour saturation. A time release or release cable also helps reduce shake.

• Ask Aboriginal people if it's OK before you take their photos.

• Carry a hand towel, insect repellent and suntan lotion (non greasy) in your camera bag.

• Be prepared to sacrifice a few photos to capture your subject (presumably human) in a more relaxed pose.

• If you're photographing a busy subject such as a group of people or part of a landscape, build your image around a distinctive feature.

• Use overcast days. They provide a soft, even light. Remember: the more contrast there is, the harder it will be for your film to capture it evenly.

• Have fun and share your tips with other photographers.

I generally travel with a 35 mm Nikon camera, a flash (which I use only when I'm desperate as I prefer shooting with natural light), and three 2.8 lenses – a 17 mm, a 35–80 zoom and a 210 mm zoom. These, along with a reflector and several filters, are stuffed mercilessly into a backpack-style camera bag. I also carry a tripod and a 6X7, medium format Pentax with a 20 mm lens which I use mainly for landscapes.

Believe me, when you're walking over hill and dale, you won't want to be carrying any more.

ARLTUNGA

Standing amid the ruins of Arltunga in summer with the sun blazing down on you and a hot, dry wind fanning your face, it's easy to imagine the hardship experienced by the hopefuls who came in search of gold in the late 1800s.

Australia, at the time, had been plunged into economic depression. Work was scarce, with husbands forced to leave their families in search of an income; markets had collapsed, forcing many farmers to leave their land. In the soup queues of the major centres, hungry, desperate men heard of vast riches to be found in the Centre – rubies by the handful and rivers of gold.

So, with the last of their meagre savings, they bought picks and shovels and caught the next train to Oodnadatta, from where they pushed their wheelbarrow with few possessions 600 kilometres through some of Australia's most unhospitable terrain to arrive at what must have seemed like hell on earth. The parched, hardened landscape delivered little water –

Above: Arltunga Police Station (that's the gaol out back, not the toilet).
Left: The MacDonnell Ranges **Next Page:** One of the restored houses at the Arltunga Historical Precinct.

barely enough to drink, let alone use for mining or washing, the cost of food staples, such as flour and tinned beef which they could barely afford anyway, were double the price anywhere else, and temperatures often topped 40 degrees – sometimes for more than 30 days in a row. Added to the heat and the freezing cold of night came sudden rains with devastating floods, making tracks impassable and adding to the extreme isolation of the field. All this before a pick was even swung to discover that the gold so desperately sought lay somewhere deep beneath the surface encased in quartz rock which was almost impervious to their equipment.

What little gold was to be found came from tunnels barely big enough to crouch in, which were laboriously dug by hand (dynamite was too expensive an option for many miners). The rock relinquished by the tunnels was carted miles to a government battery, which, without water, was the only way the rock could be crushed in large enough quantities. Lengthy delays in the battery's operation taunted the miners but still they toiled, sliding further into debt in the process. Alcohol – a luxury no one could afford but few could resist – also became a problem. Then came corruption, theft and, eventually, illness as the fine dust from the mining settled into their lungs.

From 1887 – the year gold was first discovered at Arltunga – the community struggled, its miners always on the brink of uncovering a motherlode, until finally they could endure it no longer and either died or moved on. By 1902, the Centre's first town had become a ghost town.

Now a historical reserve, Arltunga provides a fascinating glimpse into a harsh time in Central Australia' s history, where you can wander the museum and ruins and descend into several of the tunnels ...before climbing back into your car for what is sure to be one of the most comfortable drives of your life.

Top Tip: Drop into the Arltunga Bush Hotel - "The Loneliest Pub in Australia" – for a handsome feed and a yarn with the locals about some of the eccentric fossickers who return looking for gold. I particularly like the one about the guy who comes back at the same time of year and stands on his circular barbecue plate at night butt naked except for a helmet with wires poking out, reaching skyward to draw energy from the cosmos. Fancy rounding the corner in your car to catch that sight in your headlights.

Ruby Gap

This is where you come to get away from it all – though it's strictly four-wheel-drive country. It's an enjoyable drive weaving your way between the hills and gorges, cruising up the dry riverbed past shady river gums and eventually arriving at where a sign suggests it's a bit dangerous to continue by car. There are plenty of places to camp and you'll certainly get a feel for what it must have been like for the early explorers out here. Annie Gorge (now called Ruby Gap) would have to be the highlight, though it's a fair old walk up the riverbed (allow about an hour), particularly on the way back after a swim.

The area has an interesting history. It's where a huge deposit of rubies was discovered which triggered the rush from the major centres that later led to the settlement of Central Australia. An entertaining tale is told of explorer and surveyor David Lindsay who discovered the rubies. It seems one of the men who accompanied him on his expedition raced in and registered mining claims on the gorge area a day ahead of Lindsay (a nice gesture after sharing several months in the saddle), who did the right thing and first completed the survey for which he'd been commissioned. Still, justice was served 18 months later when – on the brink of converting his investment into a fortune – the rubies turned out to be worthless garnets.

Right: Following the Hale River to Ruby Gap.

Chambers Pillar

"The appearance of this feature, I should imagine to be unique in Australia and it is not likely that any future explorer will ever discover so singular a monument wherewith to immortalise either himself or his patron."

- Ernest Giles, 1872

While Giles wrote eloquently about Chambers Pillar, it was John Stuart who first sighted and named it about 12 years earlier. From then, until the advent of the railway in 1920, the Pillar became the singular landmark for travellers heading north from Adelaide. It's hard not to be moved by the solitude and history that surrounds the Pillar, particularly at sunset or later, when it is silhouetted against the night sky and moon. I'd recommend a camp out if you're travelling by four-wheel-drive, two nights if you have the time, just to take in the landscape and appreciate how welcome the sight of this lonely, 50 metre tower of sandstone must have been to the early travellers. (It will also give you the chance to curse the vandals who have added their signatures to its base).

Left: Chambers Pillar at sunrise.

Aborigines call Chambers Pillar *Itirkawara* (pronounced It-turk-kar-wara) after a Dreamtime lizard ancestor. Legend has it Itirkawara was a fierce and bad-tempered warrior who celebrated his many conquests by taking a woman outside of his own skin group and was banished to the desert for his indiscretion. When he stopped to rest he turned into the prominent formation. The Pillar (some suggest it represents his male organ) stands as a warning to all Aborigines to observe strict tribal social codes.

The visit to Chambers Pillar gives the traveller pause to consider the whole desert experience – a fitting finale for those who make it the last stop in their adventure to the Centre.

Left: Desert landscape surrounding Chambers Pillar

Recommended itinerary

Given all the options, choosing the ideal itinerary for a visit to the Centre is not easy. Your route is likely to be decided by the time you've allowed, the transport you've got, weather conditions and, of course, your interest. Remarkably, given the distance involved, the average visit to the entire Northern Territory is just 5.2 days. However, to do the Centre justice, I think you need at least a couple of weeks. Assuming you've come in your own transport this is my recommended itinerary for a comfortable 14 day visit to the Centre which will see you taking in most of the highlights:

As Uluṟu tends to overshadow any visit to the Centre, I'd head there first and spend three days taking it in and visiting Kata Tjuṯa. Then I'd leave around midday and head for Kings Canyon for two nights for some spectacular walks. Assuming you're in a four wheel drive, I'd leave early morning and make my way along the Mereenie Loop Road to Hermannsburg for lunch, then double back for two nights at the Finke National Park for some light off-road adventure. A leisurely drive to the West Macs is next, with a camp out at Redbank Gorge or a stopover at Glen Helen before heading back to Alice along the gorge swimming circuit of Namatjira Drive. Two nights in Alice is enough to relax, cruise the shops and take in a few attractions, then I'd head out to the East Macs to Trephina Gorge or Arltunga for the night – Ruby Gap if you're keen to get even further away from it all (and if you're out that far, you may as well stay another night). Then it's back to Alice either overnight or for a quick resupply before heading down to Chambers Pillar or thereabouts for two nights. On your way out of the Centre north or south, I'd plan to overnight at the Devils Marbles or Rainbow Valley where you're likely to end the holiday with some memorable photos of your visit.

Note: If I were not in a four-wheel-drive, I'd plan to do as much of this route as I could on the sealed road. I'd base myself in Alice and join a tour operator for the highlights that most interested me.

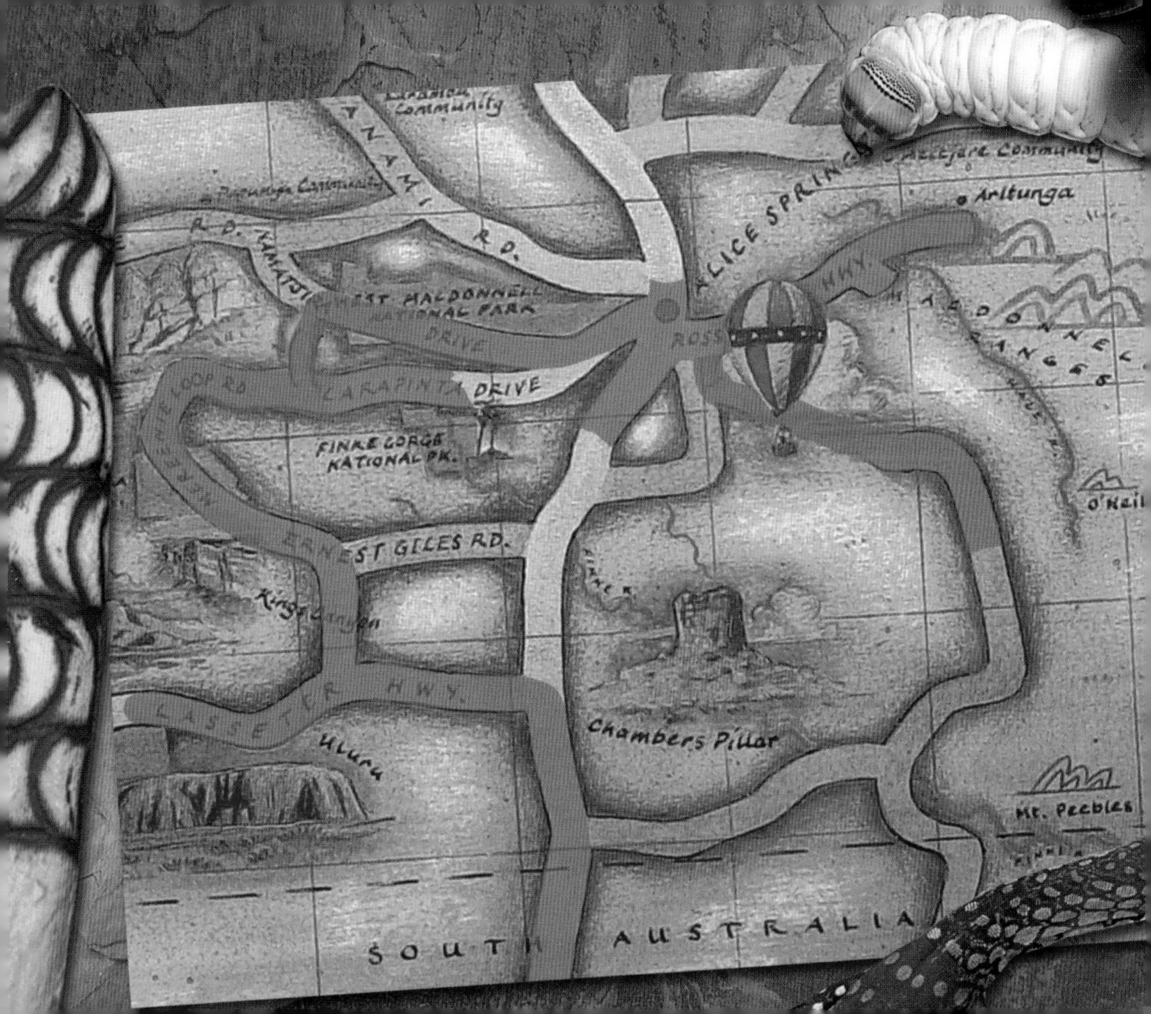
Community
TANAMI RD.
ALICE SPRINGS
Arltunga
WEST MACDONNELL NATIONAL PARK
ROSS
HWY.
MACDONNELL RANGES
LARAPINTA DRIVE
FINKE GORGE NATIONAL PK.
ERNEST GILES RD.
Kings Canyon
LASSETER HWY.
Uluru
Chambers Pillar
Mt. Peebles
SOUTH AUSTRALIA

The Author

David Kirkland is a full-time travel writer and photographer specialising, in Australia South-east Asia and the South Pacific. A journalist, photographer and author with more than 10 years experience in the tourism industry, he travelled the world extensively before settling in Brisbane, Queensland.

The Pocket Guide to The Red Centre is one of several books David has written and photographed. His coffee table book *Impressions of Papua New Guinea* and *Papua New Guinea -- The Last Great Frontier* are considered essential reading for anyone visiting the country. His Pocket Guide series is proving a popular addition to his stable of travel and souvenir publications.

Some of the author's lesser known milestones include interviewing a zombie, captaining a 40m shrimp trawler down the Amazon River and being savaged by Michael Parkinson in an interview as a cadet journalist ("I'm sure I read somewhere that the ratings of your new show were plummeting...").

David is based in Brisbane and is working on a series of travel publications throughout Australia, Asia and the South Pacific.

David Kirkland

Index of place names and prominent features

Thank you

There are several people I'd like to thank who have contributed to the making of this book. Henry Boegheim and his wife Margaret of Hema Maps in Brisbane have proved to be excellent partners in this venture. Without their support and confidence in the Pocket Guide series, this book may never have eventuated.

Again, thanks to Tim and Christina of TT Digital who faithfully scanned and digitally reproduced my images and provided much-needed technical support.

I'd also like to thank my friends Glenys and Linda who have been a constant source of encouragement throughout the process.

During the research phase of this project there were several people, in particular, who I'd like to thank for the insight they gave me. Kate Podger of the Ikuntji Women's Centre, and Alice, Eunice, Daisy and Linda, for taking me hunting on what proved to be one of the most enjoyable days I had in the Centre. I'd also like to thank Steve Fox and Walter Pukutiwara of the Maruku Art and Craft Centre, who went out of their way to help me capture images of Uluru which particularly excited me. Thanks also to Alice Springs photographer Steve Strike for his tips on shooting the Red Centre and listening to my frustration at having to deal with the ludicrous restrictions on professional photographers at Uluru.

I'm also indebted to the tourism operators who helped me, particularly the guys at Professional Helicopter Services, and the staff of Central Australian Tourism which assisted with access and checked the book for accuracy. Thanks also to Malcolm Lindsay for the great illustrative maps.

Finally, I'd like to thank my son Daniel whose enthusiasm for hearing about his father's adventures, and his keenness to one day share them, is an absolute delight to return to.

To you all, my sincere thanks.

Feedback

I'm planning to update and expand this book with interesting information and advice for future travellers to the Red Centre, so any helpful suggestions you may have would be gratefully received.

Please take the time to send them in. It's always good to receive feedback, and your observations and comments could make a big difference to someone else's holiday in the Centre. I'll publish the best of what's received in the next edition and send a complimentary copy of the next book to those whose letters are included.

David Kirkland
P.O. Box 466
Coorparoo
Brisbane Qld
Australia. 4151
E-mail: Frontierpub@bigpond.com.au.
http/www.kirklandphotos.com

Published books in the Pocket Guide Series

The Pocket Guide to Western Australia's Pilbara Region

New books planned

The Pocket Guide to the Northern Territory's Top End
The Pocket Guide to Western Australia's Kimberley Region
The Pocket Guide to Tasmania
The Pocket Guide to South Western Australia
The Pocket Guide to South East Queensland

To order

Contact Hema Maps
P.O. Box 4365 Eight Mile Plains
Brisbane, Queensland Australia. 4113
Fax: 61 7 3340 0099
E-mail: manager@hemamaps.com.au
www.hemamaps.com.au

The Pocket Guide

Travel Book Series

Notes

Notes

Notes

The Pocket Guide

Travel Book Series